Praise for *The Curse of Lovely*

'Insightful, courageous and humorous – what a wonderful addition to the self-help genre! *The Curse of Lovely* is unpretentious and rich with well-developed case studies that take the reader from compassionate self-awareness to effective change. I have found this book to be like an intimate therapy session where you learn to unpack and challenge the curse of lovely. I am sure it will become the go-to resource for all of us who struggle to say no.'

Dr F. Jay McClellan, MSc, PsychD.

'Through *The Curse of Lovely*, Jacqui Marson takes you on a journey – a journey of gentle, compassionate self-discovery. It answers the what, the how and the why in an utterly charming and non-judgemental way. It then subtly guides you into understanding and learning how to change the aspects of yourself that cause you the most misery.

The progressive use of case studies and real-life experiences make this book incredibly readable and accessible. The humorous and almost self-deprecating Jacqui shows you how to understand yourself and your behaviour without the critical "inner voice". Like a true, good therapist Jacqui guides you towards change until you get to the point of cathartic liberation from your "curse".

I loved reading this book not only because I recognised so many truths in Jacqui's observations, but because, as a fellow psychologist, I know intuitively that this book will help people

reframe their curse as a gift they can finally control and be proud of.

Buy this book if you suspect you have the curse; also buy it for anyone in your life you think has the curse of lovely – it will genuinely be a gift that keeps giving.'

Pia Sinha, Chartered Psychologist and
Deputy Governor, HM Prison Service

'The Curse of Lovely is an empowering and enlightening guide to positive change for people who struggle to stand up for themselves. Read it and be cursed no more by the weight of other people's expectations! Step into your true self with Jacqui Marson as your warm and wise companion – she offers creative and practical help to ensure you thrive in your own right.'

Val Sampson, coach and couples counsellor,
author of Tantra: The Art of Mind-blowing Sex,
and co-author of The Breast Cancer Book

'People-pleasers – read this book and you will emerge from your chrysalis of falsehood! The first real guide to setting people-pleasers free – innovative, practical, a guide to replacing niceness with authenticity.'

Oliver James, Clinical Psychologist,
author and broadcaster

The Curse of Lovely

how-to break-free-from the-demands-of others

AND LEARN TO SAY NO

JACQUI MARSON

piatkus

To the memory of my dear cousin
Debbie Marson (1957–2009), who
encouraged me to write.

PIATKUS

First published in Great Britain in 2013 by Piatkus

A CIP catalogue record for this book
is available from the British Library.

ISBN 978-0-7499-5722-3

Typeset in Sabon by M Rules
Printed and bound in Great Britain by
Clays Ltd, St Ives plc

Papers used by Piatkus are from well-managed forests
and other responsible sources.

MIX
Paper from
responsible sources
FSC www.fsc.org FSC® C104740

Piatkus
An imprint of
Little, Brown Book Group
100 Victoria Embankment
London EC4Y 0DY

An Hachette UK Company
www.hachette.co.uk

www.piatkus.co.uk

Jacqui Marson is a chartered counselling psychologist. She has worked in a variety of clinical settings in London, including Holloway Prison and St Thomas' Hospital, and currently has a successful private practice in Covent Garden. She runs workshops and training for individuals and companies around the world in communication skills, confidence and team-building.

She is also a trained journalist and is in demand by the media as a popular communicator on psychology. She regularly appears on BBC and commercial radio and television programmes, including ITV's *Lorraine* and Channel Five News. She has written for *The Psychologist* and *The Counselling Psychology Review* and had a monthly column, Fast Therapy, in *Psychologies* magazine.

Jacqui is a member of the British Psychological Society and the Health Professions Council. Her professional qualifications include B.Sc. (Hons) Psychology, M.Sc. Counselling Psychology and C. Psychol.

She lives in London with her husband and two sons.

For further information visit www.jacquimarson.co.uk

CONTENTS

ACKNOWLEDGEMENTS

I would like to thank the following people:

My talented mum, who introduced me to creativity and hard work; and my fun-loving dad, probably the first Curse of Lovely in my life.

Professor Rachel Tribe at the University of East London and my two wonderful supervisors, Dr Lynne Jordan and Dr Grace McClurg, who have all believed in me as a counselling psychologist and a human being. Vagelis Dimitrious and all the lovely staff and therapists at Neal's Yard Therapy Rooms, Covent Garden, for keeping on top of my complicated diary and supporting my practice; Anna Sternberg, Lotta Kitchen and Alex Segal of my peer supervision group, and Val Sampson, Melanie Chweyden, Laura Bond and Pia Sinha who have all given me invaluable support, encouragement, inspiration and feedback. Claudia Stumpfl, Rachel Harrison, Jules Williamson, Jacs Palmer, Orianna Fielding, Leanne Darcy,

Nathalie Salaun, Kate Eadie, Hilary Lewis, Lisa O'Kelly, Evelyn Gavshon, Julie Kleeman, Sue Charkin, Laura Solomans, Sonia Scott, Caroline Lees and Helen Fletcher for their unfailing friendship, support and encouragement. Helen Purvis and all at Knight Ayton Management for being fantastic agents, and Mary Bekhait at Limelight for negotiating the contract. Jana Sommerlad for helping me believe in good karma and my Piatkus editors Anne Lawrance and Jillian Stewart for modelling 'Lovely, with Choice' with their calm, thoughtful, straight-forward communications. Also my copy-editor Anne Newman for her patience and perseverance.

All the lovely ladies at the Delice cafe in Swiss Cottage Library who kept me going through the long winter months of writing with baked potatoes, home-made cake and warm smiles. And Steve, Mags, Lewis, Alex, Rachel, Helen, Tony, Louis and Felix for being their lovely selves ...

Finally, I would like to thank my amazing sons for their humour and help: Jess for getting me out of my technology scrapes ('don't cry mum, I've found the file') and Tom for engaging with the ideas with generosity and energy. Finally, to my husband Stewart, for embracing the housework, his editor's eye, and unconditional love.'

What *is* the Curse of Lovely?

S hortly after my forty-fifth birthday, something happened which helped me realise that I was suffering badly from the Curse of Lovely, and, if I didn't find a way to break it, then it would end up breaking me ...

My husband and I had dutifully gone along to my cousin's daughter's thirtieth birthday party. Although it was being held in a church hall two hours' drive away from where we live, I was determined to enjoy it as I am very fond of these relatives and I love a good barn dance, which is what it was to be. At about 11pm, with hardly any alcohol in my body, I galloped (the technical word) enthusiastically down the middle of two lines of participants, only to slip at the end of the line and fall over. There was quite a loud noise as I hit the floor; I don't know how to describe it – maybe a thud, or even a crack – but it was loud enough to draw gasps from the lines of dancers and several concerned enquiries of 'Are you all right?' I, of course, leapt from the hard floor to my feet, trilling, 'I'm fine, I'm fine' in a cheerful voice, and 'Carry on!'

I then danced the next three dances, despite feeling a bit nauseous from shock, and drove home, *because it was my turn.* My arm throbbed and it was painful every time I changed gear, but I thought that it would feel better in the morning. When I woke up my arm was stiff and achy, but I didn't seriously consider going to get it checked out. I didn't want to waste the time of the hardworking A&E staff – and besides, I was brought up not to make a fuss.

As it was the school holidays, I spent the next ten days taking the kids to planned activities, including driving 200 miles to visit a friend in Somerset where we went rowing on a lake. I had told her my arm was badly bruised and painful and she urged me not to take my turn at the oars, but for some crazed, 'Lovely' reason, I insisted that it was only fair. This led to what I consider to be an iconic photograph which captures the pure madness at the heart of my beliefs and behaviour. The caption would read: Jacqui rowing with a broken arm (and still smiling).

When I finally went to my local A&E they didn't chastise me for wasting their time, but seemed genuinely puzzled that someone would override the messages from their own body for so long. 'You did this ten days ago?' they kept repeating, shaking their heads with bemusement. (Just to reassure you, it wasn't one of those breaks where the bone is actually sticking out – even I am not that bad. I had fractured the radius at the elbow joint.) They gave me a bright blue sling, so at last I had permission to not use that arm, now that the world could see that I was officially injured, as opposed to just (the forbidden) making a fuss or malingering. I could now sidestep the obviously impossible task of asking for what I needed in a clear and direct way myself. Instead, my beautiful sling told people: this woman has a broken arm – help her!

My stepdaughter, a family ally and herself no stranger to the Curse of Lovely, sent me a text message saying: Step away from the stake, Joan of Arc. I thought this was hilarious and very insightful. Basically, I realised that if I carried on being such a martyr and consistently putting the needs of others before my own, something a lot worse than a broken arm might happen to me.

That day, I contacted a therapist I had wanted to work with for ten years, and took my first tentative steps towards beginning to break the Curse (and planting the seeds of this book). I have learnt so much from my own process, as well as from working with my therapy clients in my own practice in London – many of whom have generously allowed me to share their stories with you in this book. I feel privileged that they have let me into their lives and struggles.

WHO IS THIS BOOK FOR?

The three questions I am most frequently asked about breaking the Curse of Lovely are:

1. Is it just for attractive people (and what do *they* have to worry about?)

2. Surely we don't want people to be *less* nice in this world?

3. Is this just a problem for women?

Firstly, what I refer to as 'Lovely' has nothing to do with physical appearance; it is not about looking pretty, beautiful or handsome. It is about *being* lovely – behaving in ways that other people will often refer to as lovely, as in, 'Ah, he/she's such a lovely person'.

To answer question number two, this book is not aimed at people who might need to work on being nicer in their day-to-day lives. It is aimed at people whose default response is always to be nice (kind, compassionate, pleasing, etc.) to the extent that this has come to feel problematic to them. If you are at a point in your life where you feel trapped by a lack of choice of ways to think, communicate and behave other than 'niceness', then this book is for you.

In answer to question number three, no, this is not just a problem for women. You probably all know at least one man who people refer to as 'lovely', and my hunch would be that that feels as trapping and problematic to him as it does to all the Lovely women.

In my fifteen years of clinical experience as a Chartered Counselling Psychologist I have seen many women *and* men's lives, relationships, careers and wellbeing blighted by the belief that to be liked, loved and accepted they have to limit themselves to behaviours they feel are approved of by others. These might include some or all of the following: always being polite, nice, helpful, charming, fun, making people feel good about themselves, not letting people down, never saying no, avoiding conflict and putting others' needs before their own.

I decided to name this the Curse of Lovely as it is indeed a paradox: most people would like to be known as lovely, but for these individuals, it feels like a curse put on them at birth by a wicked witch. They are trapped, suffocated and oppressed by the weight of others' expectations and feel that change is not an option. Lovelies believe that expressing their own needs will mean being rejected and not loved, and they therefore suppress the expression of many important parts of themselves, including feelings such as anger and resentment, which then simmer inside. No one else is aware of this because they always appear to be agreeable and smiling. Then one day the Lovely person explodes and everyone is shocked. The Lovely person feels disapproved of, thus fulfilling their own unhelpful belief that their anger is unacceptable to others. And so the cycle (or 'Curse') is perpetuated.

This book suggests ways in which you can, gently, begin to break the Curse of Lovely, set yourself free from the stifling expectations of others and live a more complete and fulfilling life.

HOW TO USE THIS BOOK

I always find it is best to start in very small ways, as success is a brilliant reinforcing experience and encourages us to try more. But please feel free to use the book in any way that works for you. Someone joked to me that as a perfectionist high achiever she would go straight to Chapter Nine to try the Advanced Behavioural Experiments. That, of course, is great, if it is what you want to do. There are no rules. But I would suggest reading the whole book and seeing what resonates with you; if everyone has one new thought or tries one new thing, I would be delighted, as I know that is how I have gained most from my favourite self-help books. I then tend to go back to them time and time again, usually gaining a new insight, idea or resource. It might also be helpful to use a notebook to keep track of useful ideas, thoughts and insights that come to you while reading the book. But, of course, if you hate that idea, don't do it!

You might also find that while working through this book you'll want to talk through some of the issues raised either with a trusted friend or relative, or think about contacting a therapist to go further with this work (see Resources, page 218, for information on contacting a therapist).

Good luck – and remember, this is not an Olympic ice-dance competition, and no one is scoring your performance. Treat your experience with compassionate curiosity and I hope you might even have a bit of lightness and fun along the way.

CHAPTER ONE

A Day in the Life of a Cursed Lovely

Let's take a look at a hypothetical day in the life of a cursed Lovely to help you see if you identify with this idea.

The Lovely person wakes up and, in an ideal world, would like to make some tea, listen to the radio, take a shower, get dressed, eat breakfast then go to work or get on with the day. In a complete fantasy world, they might dream of lingering over one or all of these tasks: maybe slowly brewing a beautiful pot of favourite leaf tea, relaxing in a scented bubble bath, carefully choosing some clothes that they know will make them feel happy and confident, picking the right shoes that will match, yet be comfortable ... But a small (or not so small) person is calling out, 'Where's my blue jumper?' while another wants to know why there is no milk left in the fridge, an auntie has just rung to ask him/her to pop in to visit his/her nan as 'she's on her own, poor thing', and a friend has sent a text expressing a desperate need to talk as her boyfriend has not returned her calls for twenty-four hours.

Within minutes of waking, not only is any element of the fantasy version laughable, but the Lovely person is already overriding his or her own basic needs in order to take care of those of others. On any given morning they can easily leave the house having eaten no breakfast, wearing the shoes that pinch their big toes and with dry shampoo in their hair – hungry, hassled and a bit scuzzy, but comforting themselves with the thought that they have looked after everyone else and kept them happy. Others' potential bad moods have been avoided, and there's been no shouting or cross faces in the house. And, on a deeper (and probably subconscious) emotional level, they feel safe and that they will be loved because they have looked after everyone else. Or, maybe, that they will not get into trouble because they have not let anyone down.

CHANGE IS POSSIBLE

We are, of course, not all the same shade of Lovely. There are many different manifestations for different types of Lovely in different situations; but the similarity will be that we often feel completely overwhelmed by the expectations of others and have absolutely no idea of how to behave any other way. In fact, the very thought of doing so, for example refusing a request, is usually terrifying. We create expectations, and then, at some point, feel terribly trapped by them – the skills which have helped to create the expectation usually being the very opposite of those we need to change it.

Indira, who you will meet again in Chapter Six , described how her family treated her as an 'open-all-hours' commodity, who would be expected to drop everything to let the plumber in to their rental properties, make their dentist appointments and provide bed, breakfast and the face of success to relatives visiting from the home country. As the only unmarried daughter, she foresaw, with utter dread, a future of caring for one or both ailing parents, while feeling a 'bad, ungrateful daughter' for having these thoughts and panicking because she had neither the time nor energy left to meet any men to save her from her unmarried-daughter fate.

As you will see with the other clients' stories in this book, there is no easy, overnight answer. Our patterns of thought, emotion and behaviour have usually been in place for most of our lives and have often served us well – until the point where they no longer do; the point where, we could say they transform from being our friend to being our foe.

The way to change is by taking small, manageable steps – just a few at a time – designed with the understanding that this is a brave and terrifying thing that we are trying to do for ourselves. Indira experimented with the guiding metaphor that she would no longer be a twenty-four/seven convenience store, but could shut up shop at certain times – maybe more like a 7-Eleven (the original late-night stores, open 7am to 11pm). Now that might still seem a lot of opening hours, but to try and go straight away to being a strict 9am–5pm business would have been too great a change both for Indira and for her friends and family.

As the family therapist and writer Harriet Lerner says, if you try and change too much too quickly, the behaviour of those around you will scream 'Change back!' and it will become a self-defeating exercise.

HOW THE CURSE OF LOVELY WORKS

Let's go back to the story of my broken arm (see page 1) to see what that tells us about how the Curse actually works – how it often begins and how it maintains itself through a lifetime.

Essentially we all have layers upon layers of rules that we adhere to – what we could call 'Personal Rules' or 'Rules for Living'. Different rules are taught and reinforced by different social agencies in our lives, from parents and relatives to teachers, caregivers, then later employers and agencies of the state, such as the police and government. Some are clearly enshrined in law, and if you break them there is a penalty to pay. And some, such as 'Don't play with matches' or 'Look both ways before you cross the road' are taught to us at a young age to keep us safe. But the more tricky ones often sit in our subconscious. Placed there by parents or caregivers at an early age, these rules can exert a huge amount of power, and yet we rarely bring them out into the light of day (i.e. our current adult reality) and examine them to see if we still choose to live by them – in short, whether or not they are still *helpful* to us, to who we are now and to the way we want to live our lives. If we did examine them, we might well find that some (or many) are stuck in a dichotomous all-or-nothing mode – they have lost all flexibility and become what Cognitive Behavioural Therapy (CBT) founder Aaron Beck called 'Rigid Personal Rules'. You can spot a Rigid Personal Rule if you are using words such as 'should', 'must', 'always', 'never' (we will look at this in more detail in Chapter Five). Throughout this book I have put people's 'Rigid Personal Rules' in small capitals so that you can identify them easily.

So in the broken-arm story, my rule of NEVER MAKE A FUSS was, in fact, a Rigid Personal Rule. It was so powerful (despite being half-hidden in my subconscious) that I could override serious pain signals from my body and still muster the energy to reassure others ('I'm fine. I'm fine!'), plaster a smile on my face, keep dancing, not seek medical assistance for ten days *and* go rowing.

This rule undoubtedly has its roots in childhood: if a child hurts themselves and starts crying, their mum might say, 'Oh don't make such a fuss' (disapproval) or, conversely, if they are able to shrug it off and carry on, praise them for being 'a big brave soldier' (approval). Like Pavlov's dogs which were 'conditioned' to salivate when they heard a bell ring signalling food, even when no food appeared, small children can be conditioned fairly easily to continue behaviours that are rewarded (by praise, approval or gold stars) and discontinue those that are criticised, disapproved of or punished. In the last decade, popular communication of scientific research – via anything from the *Supernanny* television programmes to widely available parenting-skills training and books – has taught parents, teachers and carers to reward the desired behaviours and ignore the undesired. But in my day – and still in many cultures today – children were often ridiculed, shamed, humiliated or punished for what were seen as undesirable traits and behaviours.

Breaking the rules

I'm not blaming my own or any other parents here. They did what they thought was best, and usually this is a version of how they were parented themselves, passing on those rules that were consciously or unconsciously taught to them. Certain behaviours and traits are 'privileged' in different family systems, meaning that there are beliefs – which may go back generations – that some ways of being and behaving are better than others.

In my family, I think it is fair to say that 'toughness' was privileged. In this hierarchy of behaviour, it could be argued that one of my finest hours as a horse-mad kid, was when aged six, I was thrown off a lively pony in a large field of newly cut straw. One foot got stuck in a stirrup and I was dragged over the stubble field for at least ten minutes, my back scratched and bleeding from the cut stalks. I can't remember if I cried – I'm sure I did – but what we all remember is that I got back on the horse and rode again, even though I must have been very frightened. This tale is told with tacit approval in my family as something of a 'Hero story', so, understandably, I internalised it as something positive about myself that I should develop (while at the same time, trying to suppress the 'weak' little girl who might cry at such times).

An important idea here is that as well as looking at what these internalised rules may have come to cost us, we can take a step back and see what we may have gained from them. So on the one hand, I can say, 'Look how this poor little girl was taught to override physical pain and be brave at all costs', but on the other, I have to acknowledge that a large part of my early career as a war reporter was probably built on this training. I could be in extreme desert heat, sub-zero Arctic temperatures, go without food or drink, carry heavy equipment, dodge bullets, and I don't think I ever complained. I would usually be smiling and 'bubbly' and looking after everyone around me, cracking jokes and making them feel good about themselves. When we are nice, kind and giving and everyone seems to love us, then it is important to recognise that this is something we have gained from our behaviour. But when the price becomes too high – in terms of our exhaustion, resentment, suppressed anger or lack of self-care – we have to be prepared to let go of some of the old safety of those gains.

This is, of course, much easier said than done. We have to build confidence in new ways of doing things, before we can even *think* of abandoning some of the old, safe ways – even once we have realised the price they are extracting.

Parenthood seems to exacerbate any tendencies we have towards a Loveliness that is problematic to ourselves. Qualities which can underpin the feeling – eventually – of being cursed, such as kindness, selfless giving, nurturing and putting others' needs before our own, are all exalted in our contemporary idealisation of the perfect parent (especially mothers). Many women don't feel that their Loveliness is a curse until they are many years into mothering children and realise that what they once gave freely and lovingly is now taken for granted and expected by others.

SUSIE'S LOVELY DAY

Susie has four children aged between five and thirteen. After Susie's dad died when she was eight years old, her mother raised six children alone and worked in three jobs, day and night, to make ends meet. So maternal attention was in short supply, and the kids had to be self-sufficient from an early age. Although Susie admires her mum enormously for her hard work, determination and sacrifice, she wants to give her own children all the attention and loving support she feels she missed and so has chosen to be a stay-at-home mum. This, of course, is a job that demands its own levels of hard work, determination and sacrifice – although it is rarely acknowledged as such. Here is a day from Susie's life. It is extreme, but typical in many ways.

Susie woke at 6am to walk the dog, make breakfast and pack lunches, before doing the school run then rushing to a school fundraising committee meeting. As she was leaving the meeting her phone rang. It was an estate agent reminding her that new tenants were moving in to her mother's flat in three days' time and asking if she'd managed to buy new wardrobes for them? Feeling guilty and caught out, she grabbed her coat and car keys and immediately drove to Ikea where she piled her trolley up with heavy flat-pack wardrobes and joined a long, slow queue at the checkout. While she was queuing and fretting about how she would load the heavy packs, and when on earth she would find time to assemble them, her phone rang again. This time it was two dear old friends she had arranged to meet for lunch. The date had been made months earlier as the friends lived out of town and it was the only one they could all fit into their busy schedules. 'I hadn't forgotten, because only the day before I was looking at my diary and thinking how much I was looking forward to seeing them. But in the panic of dealing with the agent's call, I had just blanked it from my mind,' she told me later in our therapy session.

The panicky feelings compounded as the day progressed and Susie tried to do everything and please everyone. She ended up rushing to the lunch over an hour late, trying to squeeze into a tight parking space and backing out and crashing into a parked taxi. This terrible, over-scheduled day carried on with more frantic rushing around collecting kids, delivering kids, cooking tea and supervising homework, until Susie was forced to go to bed, shivering and vomiting with what she realised was probably delayed shock and exhaustion. 'It was my own fault,' she said. Then smiling ruefully, she added, 'I should have said no.'

'What Rigid Personal Rules do you think governed those choices?' I asked her, compassionately, because so many women I know would have done the same, and if we judge ourselves harshly, then that is just another undermining layer of disempowerment and self-flagellation.

Susie identified that a key rule for her is I MUST ALWAYS DO AS I AM TOLD BY AUTHORITY FIGURES. She could see that this came from her childhood where the house was run like a military campaign by her overstretched mother, and woe betide anyone who questioned authority. She also highlighted another classic Lovely rule: I MUST ALWAYS HELP OTHERS, BUT I CAN'T ASK FOR HELP. What I often say to myself and to clients is: think of someone you like and admire and ask yourself what would they do in this situation? Susie has an Australian friend, Kat, who is very straightforward and assertive. 'What would Kat have done?' I asked her. She laughed. 'She would have told the agents to get off her back, that she would sort it at her own convenience, then gone and enjoyed the lunch. And she probably would have asked someone if they could pick up her kids so she could enjoy it for longer and not be rushed. She might even have had a glass of wine!'

SO HOW DO WE LEARN TO SAY NO?

For Indira and Susie, feeling oppressed by the needs and expectations of others, the most simple thing would appear to be to learn how to say no more often. This is what friends and critics alike advise us. However, we know this advice so well that it has become internalised into what I call a 'self-beating *should*' (we will look at this more in Chapter Five). Note how Susie smiled ruefully and said, 'I should have said no'. 'What are you thinking?' I asked her in the therapy session. 'What does that expression on your face signify?'

Susie could barely bring herself to speak. Finally, she said in a very small voice: 'I guess I feel ashamed that I can't stand up for myself. I make a funny story out of it, but really I am thinking – why *can't* I say no? I'm an intelligent woman. I even did some assertiveness training once, so I know the theory. I even role-played the skills ... I *should* be able to do it. But I can't. And that makes me feel a total failure ...' she trailed off and looked miserably at the floor.

We will hear about Susie's progress later in the book. But for now, this example helps to illustrate why learning new skills *alone* is probably not enough for most readers who identify with the concept of a cursed Lovely. It is important that we also look at the feelings and thoughts that sit intertwined with our behaviours. A simple way of understanding this is to look at the diagram below, which shows that our thoughts, feelings and behaviour are interlinked. Each affects the other, and therefore, theoretically, we can change our *pattern* by changing any one side of this triangle.

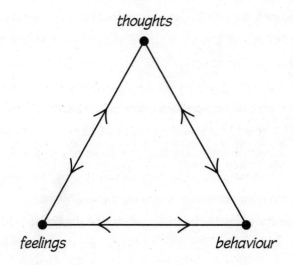

Over the years, I have come to realise that there is no rule as to the *best* side of the triangle to start working on with clients who want to change patterns they feel trapped in. Therapy as I practise it, is a collaborative process in which the client is the expert on their own life, and the therapist brings skills, experience and a different perspective. Some people want to jump straight in and *do* something different, while others prefer to look back into their past to see what formed particular patterns. Mostly, it is not a straightforward, linear process for anyone, and clients will move backward and forward in their journey of insight, understanding and change, weaving together understanding and questioning of old thinking, while learning and trying out new skills and ways of doing things.

SUMMARY

This chapter has introduced the idea that you do not have to feel trapped by other people's expectations that you will always behave in Lovely ways. You can break free from this pattern.

- Focus on making small, manageable changes.

- Think about how your thoughts, feelings and behaviour are interlinked – see the diagram on page 17.

- Be compassionate to yourself on this journey of change and allow for steps backward as well as forward.

CHAPTER TWO

How It All Begins – the Lovely Child

Despite what your doting nan may tell you, no one is born Lovely. You may have been an early smiler, a calm, contented baby or had big brown eyes, long dark lashes and a thick head of hair which people cooed over as you lay in your pram. But Lovely, as we are talking about it here, is not about the physical attributes bestowed upon you by your DNA. The Curse of Lovely is a collection of beliefs and behaviours that have become problematic to you, and which you would like to change. Now the good news here is that beliefs and behaviour are *learned*. And therefore, because they are learned, they can be unlearned, or more precisely, *re*learned in ways that are more helpful and less costly to your health, happiness and wellbeing.

THE COMPLEX WORLD OF THE CHILD

Most of our deeply held beliefs about who we are and how we should behave originated in childhood, often before our capacity for rational thought had developed, so we tended to believe everything that we were told or experienced.

Going home on the bus last night I was fascinated to watch two different toddlers as they sat in their buggies. One was a little girl aged about eighteen months old. She was very curious about everything around her, not least the bright pink laces on her cute little trainers. She was fascinated by them, touching the curve of the bows and the hard bits on the ends, exploring the differences in shape and texture, learning about her world experientially – exactly what a toddler's job is, as the wonderfully compassionate 'Toddler Tamer' Dr Christopher Green would say. Her mother (or it might have been her nanny) seemed enthralled by her, constantly smiling down and making little noises of encouragement. Then, inevitably, the little girl managed to untie first one lace and then the other. Next step – pulling a shoe off! A look of utter amazement and pleasure lit up her face as she grasped her trophy in her pudgy little fingers. You could tell by the look on her face that she wasn't being 'naughty' – she was exploring, and the mother/nanny took it as such and said, in a warm, calm tone, something like: 'Clever girl! But let's put it back on now cos we have to get off the bus.' She then put the shoe back on and did the laces up with a complete absence of anger or stress in her movements. 'Ahh yes,' I can hear the harassed parents among you saying, 'definitely the nanny! Probably looking forward to clocking off at six and having a peaceful night with her boyfriend.' And those are valid thoughts that I will address in a moment.

After they got off the bus a second toddler/carer pair got on. This mother or nanny looked blank-faced and fed up. The child was a boy and slightly older – maybe two or two and a half – so he had more language and was a bit livelier. The woman was feeding him some kind of snack, piece by piece from a packet, but barely looking at him as she did so. Then she took a beaker out of her bag and tried to put it to his mouth, but he kept batting it away with his little toddler hands and shouting, 'No' (the favourite word of the two-year-old). She was clearly frustrated by this and they were soon engaged in a battle, the mum/nanny scowling and tutting loudly. Finally (before I got off the bus), I heard her hiss in a loud whisper through clenched teeth: 'You are so stupid! You'll be thirsty later and it will be your own fault.'

Now if what I witnessed is representative of those two children's everyday experience (and of course, it might not be, I just observed a moment in time), then how do you think they will grow up? What do you think they will think and feel about themselves? One has been told that he is stupid, the other has been told that she is clever. And really, at this age, the actual words spoken are the least important part of the ongoing communication between adult and child; so much will be inferred from tone of voice and body language – the smiles and warm tone that say, 'You are lovable! I am enchanted by you!' or the stressed anger that says, 'You are a pain! You make me angry!'

THE GOOD-ENOUGH PARENT

Now please don't think I am being judgmental and unre-alistic here; I know that it is impossible to be mother/nanny A in the story above all, or even most, of the time. I've got two children of my own, a stepdaughter and two step-grandchildren. I think it is the hardest job in the world and the one with perhaps the least worth attached to it in our present-day society. I had some terrible days when my boys were small, when I felt very alone, unvalued and unsupported and I was, therefore, far from warm and loving towards them. I can remember crying on that very same number 46 bus when an older woman told me off for sitting in a disabled priority seat with a toddler at my feet and a baby in my arms. 'You're not disabled,' she spat, 'you are young and fit.' And as I struggled to stand up and give her the seat (the Curse of Lovely, of course I did – *and* I apologised), I burst into tears, mumbled, 'What about mothers?' and stumbled off the bus two stops early, feeling utterly humiliated as all the other passengers watched (but no one spoke up for me). I think I then shouted at my toddler for nothing in particular because I felt angry and ashamed. So I know how hard it is to be the perfect mummy. And I also know that it is much better to aim for being 'good enough' and human, but to have an aware-ness of how our actions impact on our children – because they do.

CONDITIONAL LOVE:
I AM WHAT THEY CALL MY BEHAVIOUR

Research into infant development since the 1950s led by pioneers such as John Bowlby and D. W. Winnicott has consistently shown a strong link between how we are related to as small children and how our sense of self develops. Basically, if we are treated as if we are lovable, valuable and worthwhile, then we tend to grow up feeling (mostly) that we are lovable, valuable and worthwhile. Our core beliefs about ourselves are largely positive.

Love can be conditional or unconditional. 'Unconditional love' means that there are no conditions attached – that you are loved purely and simply because of who you are, whereas 'conditional love' means that conditions are attached: I love you *when* you do x, y or z or when you *don't do* a, b or c.

For a child, it is very hard to differentiate between who they are and what they do. If a little girl is constantly told she is a 'bad girl' for snatching her baby brother's toy truck, pulling the cat's tail or sticking her tongue out at Grandma, then she will begin to believe she *is* a bad girl. If she only gets love and affection or praise and attention when she behaves in a certain way or does certain things, then she will grow up believing she is only worthwhile when she is this way or does these things. Psychologist Carl Rogers called this developing 'conditions of worth'. What would be more helpful, however, is to tell the child that she is loved and valued, but that those *behaviours* are not, and would she please not do them in future. This form of parenting (and teaching) differentiates between behaviour – what we *do* – which can be learnt and unlearnt, and who we *are*, which is much less changeable.

Most people who suffer from the Curse of Lovely will have developed some, or many, unhelpful 'conditions of worth' when they were children.

MONIKA: THE 1000-WATT BULB

Thirty-nine-year-old Monika came to see me because she was feeling isolated and anxious. She felt she couldn't make friends like other people seemed to, and despite being in a good relationship with her partner, her social anxiety was beginning to cause friction between them, especially when she didn't want to spend time with his friends and family.

At first glance, Monika didn't seem to be an obvious sufferer from the Curse of Lovely, but as she talked to me more it became clear that the main reason she couldn't maintain friendships was because she gave so much of herself that it was exhausting and unsustainable. This was such an old, ingrained habit that Monika could not conceive of being any other way. 'I can't be with someone and not give to them,' she explained. 'I only know how to be a 1000-watt light bulb that lights everything up and lifts the mood. I have no gradation; I have to give it all or avoid the situation.'

Like many Lovelies, Monika did not regard her own energy as a precious resource that she could choose how, when and to whom she gave it. She operated to an unconscious Rigid

Personal Rule that told her: IF YOU ARE WITH ANY OTHER PERSON THEN YOU MUST GIVE THEM YOUR FULL ATTENTION AND ENERGY. As is the case with any Rigid Personal Rule I wanted to help Monika uncover the 'or else' sitting at the end of it. 'So what might happen if you weren't the 1000-watt bulb?' I asked.

Monika's body tensed and she looked terrified at my question. Usually a high-octane talker, Monika fell silent. 'What is the fear?' I persisted gently. Monika started to cry. 'It's disapproval. I can't bear it if anyone disapproves of me at all. Even strangers. I'm very sensitive to the slightest change in their body language. I constantly scan their faces and read their expressions – it's totally exhausting.'

We talked about her childhood. When Monika was three years old, her family moved to a very isolated village in the middle of the countryside. Her dad was a travelling salesman who was away a lot, and she thinks her mum became lonely and unhappy. 'There was only one bus a week to the nearest town and she loved shopping, so I think she must have been bored out of her brain and probably angry and frustrated. We took my brother to school every morning, then came home for a long six hours together. I was her little helper around the house and I remember she would get very angry and fly off the handle if I made a mistake. She would often fly into a temper and slap me for doing something wrong, like missing some dust on the sideboard. But then we had good times together too when I would sing and dance and entertain her, and she would be happy and call me her best friend and say that no one else could calm her like I could.'

'What were you scared of most,' I asked. 'Her anger or her disapproval?' 'Well, I suppose one was so linked to the other, that, as a child, I couldn't tell the difference. All I knew was that if I didn't keep her happy and entertained, then she might get mad, yell and hit me.' 'Do you think if someone disapproves of you now they might lose their temper and hit you?' I asked. Monika looked at me in amazement. 'No, of course not, that's completely ridiculous!' Then she looked thoughtful: 'Actually, maybe I do. My fear is so intense that it has to be linked to something very powerful and dramatic. But of course, I have never dared test it out as an adult, so maybe I do still believe that on some level.'

Being Lovely to survive

Children have no real power to stand up and fight, to run away or to ask others for help. There are very few actual options open to them and one of these is trying to control how they behave to bring about desired behaviours in their caretakers. So being Lovely may well feel like a matter of life-or-death survival.

For Monika, if she could please her mother, or make her happy and not angry or sad, then she would escape pain and the intensely fearful feelings that went with anticipating it. But she has carried with her into adult life an almost phobic reaction to the slightest hint of disapproval on the face of anyone – especially women – her subconscious mind linking this look to the anticipation of either physical pain or the emotional pain of rejection.

None of the events making her mother angry and unpredictable was Monika's responsibility as a small child – she did
not cause them, nor could she fix them. But before the age of
seven or eight our growing brains have very little capacity for
rational thought and we often rely on what is referred to as
'Magical Thinking' before this age. This means that we think
we can control the universe, and the behaviour of those
around us. It is why this is often the stage at which small
children can be a bit obsessive ('If I don't step on the lines in
the pavement, the bears won't get me', for example), making
deals with the universe to allay their anxieties. So can begin
Rigid Personal Rules such as: IF I AM ALWAYS GOOD AND NICE
(or careful or quiet or hardworking – this could be any number
of approved behaviours), THEN MUMMY (or daddy or big
brother) WILL BE HAPPY AND LOVING TO ME (or not shout at or
punish me). And the belief will be reinforced because *sometimes* it will work. Sometimes we will do as we're told and
be sweet and nice and good, and our caregiver *will* respond
in a loving way. Then, like a pint-sized slot-machine addict,
we will keep trying to hit the jackpot again, not understanding that our win was really quite random, and that we can't
control it by repeating the same winning strategy over and
over again. Of course, when we don't hit the jackpot and 'win'
the desired behaviour from the caregiver, we believe that we
must try harder, and that it is our fault that we are not winning
more often.

These patterns of belief and behaviour, which made good
sense and were effective in helping us get our needs met as
children, tend to continue, unexamined and untested, into

adulthood, where they serve us far less effectively and often become actively *unhelpful* in helping us be who we want to be. So for Monika, her strategy of being a high-energy entertaining presence was reasonably effective when she was very young, and one of the few options available to her for managing her mother's unpredictable anger. But now this strategy leaves her so drained and exhausted that she avoids social gatherings and is feeling lonely and friendless. My work with Monika included finding ways she could safely test out her beliefs, by constructing small, step-by-step behavioural experiments to show that the disapproval of others would not lead to violent, unmanageable or unbearable outcomes (see Chapter Eight for more about these).

ANGER AVOIDER OR APPROVAL SEEKER: WHICH KIND OF LOVELY ARE YOU?

Like Monika, many Lovelies fall into the category of Anger Avoider: we are *disproportionately* fearful of conflict, disapproval or criticism. We will usually (but not always) avoid the following: complaining in a restaurant, taking goods back to a shop, making any kind of complaint (however justified), disagreeing with someone in a debate or argument, saying no to a request or asking someone to stop (or start) doing something. We will also seek to avoid the kind of campaigning, angry person who is in every office, neighbourhood and school playground and tries to get us to share their injustice and sign their petition. These people tend to make us anxious by their mere presence, even before they have asked for the thing that we can't say no to.

On the other side of the coin to avoiding anger sits the Approval Seeker. In my experience, most people suffering from the Curse of Lovely are a combination of Anger Avoider and Approval Seeker – although for some, one strategy manifests more strongly than the other.

Like anger avoiding, approval seeking comes in many forms. Top of my own personal list would be mollifying, flattering and sympathising with the angry, ranting person in the hope that if they like me, they will stop being angry (not that they are necessarily angry with me, but the Lovely's rage-o-meter tends to be so sensitive that it is almost impossible to differentiate). Next would be seeking praise, thanks, gratitude, 'top marks' (whatever that means to you – for Samantha, below, that meant a spotless house and ironed Babygros), doing good deeds, never saying no, trying to ensure everyone likes you (or certainly that no one dislikes you), being accommodating, helpful, caring, kind, polite and unselfish. You may recognise some – or all – of these, and you may have lots of your own to add to the list. And of course, none of these behaviours is wrong per se. However, we know that they are unhelpful to us because we believe there is no alternative way of being, and therefore feel trapped within them. What we are aiming for is: Lovely, when we choose to be.

If you can make sure you are getting approval from those who actually have some power over you (your boss, for example), or more likely, as an adult, those who you have subconsciously *chosen* to given power to (your partner, friend, parent), then you will feel all is ok with the world. You will momentarily feel calm and safe and good about yourself. This is why Lovelies often have perfectionist tendencies. Take the example of Monika (see page 24): if she could do all the tasks her mother set her *perfectly*, then she might gain praise, a warm look or a hug. But if anything was slightly imperfect in her mother's eyes, then she might be yelled at, criticised, punished or ignored.

Samantha: who can give me approval now?

For Samantha, life had become very difficult since she had had her first baby at the age of thirty-five. 'I'm feeling a bit lost, I don't know who I am any more,' she told me and started crying. 'Before having Izzy I was very hardworking and ambitious, but now I'm letting things slide. I'm worried about what people think of me, my career, my appearance. I've put on weight since having the baby and I worry that my husband doesn't find me attractive.'

The transition to motherhood puts a huge strain on the self-image of most women. Many of the component parts of their identity – being good at their jobs, liking their bodies, being energetic friends or partners, having time to do the things that make them feel like themselves – usually disappear, some of them for good, some for just a short time and some to be replaced with different things, many of which they don't even know yet.

Samantha explained that she was the only child of doting

parents, who told her she was very special and could achieve anything if she worked hard enough. She was crazy about ballet and wanted to be a world-famous ballerina, dancing the lead in *Swan Lake* to thunderous applause. 'From the age of three until seventeen, I practised ballet four nights a week and at weekends too. My teacher was very strict. She really pushed me and was very withholding of her praise; if I came top in a ballet exam, the most I might get would be a faint curl of the lip, a raised eyebrow and a warning that the next exam was going to be much more challenging, so I'd better get practising!'

In our sessions, Samantha realised that she was totally driven by the need for praise, to be literally the (ballet) 'teacher's pet' in any situation. 'I actually think my work ethic comes from being a dancer. I can't underestimate the part my dance teacher played in my whole need for attention. My last boss loved me as I was always the one opening the office in the morning or closing up at night. I worked like a mad thing, but it was all to win his praise.'

Where do you seek approval?

Many of us will recognise versions of our own childhood in Samantha's story. When approval is scarce, gaining it can become addictive, as we seek it out from whatever source is available, sometimes indiscriminately.

Pioneering psychologist Carl Rogers wrote about the 'locus of evaluation', which can be predominantly internal or external and relates to whether you judge your actions, work, achievements and behaviour yourself (internal) or you are governed more by how others seem to evaluate you (external).

Of course, it varies from situation to situation, and we are all a mixture of both. But we also have to be realistic. So in the context of external exams and qualifications, for example, you won't get far if your internal locus of evaluation says you are an A-star student, but the external locus of evaluation, your GCSE results, are all Fs. Nowadays, a huge amount of external evaluation is built into our highly competitive culture, be it from seemingly endless exams to rating photographs on Facebook.

But chances are, if you suffer from the Curse of Lovely, then the external locus will be *far* stronger than your internal one. In fact, many of my clients struggle to feel *any* of their own judgment, or valuing, of themselves. They have given that judgment away to other people, and usually this habit started way back in childhood, when everything was about what they *did*, rather than who they *were*. This takes us back to the idea of conditional love, where you tend to feel loved and valued for what you do, rather than who you are.

BELIEFS FORMED IN THE SENSITIVE TEEN YEARS

Working with many clients over the years has shown me that it not just our childhood experiences of love and attachment that can set us up with beliefs and behaviours that become unhelpful in later life; I believe that what happens to us in the sensitive teenage years of growth and development can also have a powerful and long-lasting effect.

Ella: fear of the mean girls

When Ella was growing up, her father worked for a big multinational corporation and was posted to different countries for a few years at a time. Ella's experience was of starting many different schools and always feeling like the new girl, often not even able to communicate in her first language. An intelligent, fast learner, Ella doesn't remember this being particularly problematic until she reached her teenage years. 'By then I was at an American High School and it was just like the movie *Mean Girls*. There was a bunch of super-cool girls who topped the Hierarchy of Cool and they were complete and utter bitches to anyone like me who was a bit geeky, wore the wrong clothes and didn't know how to play the game. They mocked my hair, my accent and my ignorance about boys.'

Ella felt isolated and excluded and internalised the taunt of 'loser'. 'I was always in on a Saturday night, watching rubbish TV with my mum and dad. The phone never rang. Then on Monday morning they would all be gossiping about whatever party they had been to, who had got off with who, who fancied who – and I'd be excluded from this exciting-sounding world where all the boy action seemed to happen.'

Ella grew up to become a woman who is very dependent on the approval of her friends and constantly anxious about being rejected or excluded by them. If she hears of a social event she has not been invited to, she will spend days analysing what she has said and to whom, to try and work out if she might have offended someone. Ella is obsessed with fitting in with her crowd of friends, and although she can now buy her own clothes and spend money getting her hair 'right', she realises that she often feels anxious in a group and constantly monitors what she is going to say or do, so as not to stand out and attract negative attention. 'I feel exhausted by my constant vigilance. I never feel I can be myself, although I'm not even that sure who I am any more, anyway. And I never feel I can turn down any request or invite because I don't want to offend anyone.' This is all making Ella very unhappy: 'Sometimes I think I hate my life and just want to move somewhere far away and start all over again,' she told me, flatly.

Many people will empathise with Ella's feelings and her desire to escape. We will catch up with her later in the book (see Chapters Four and Eight) to see how she has sought to reconnect with her true self, strengthen her internal locus of evaluation and become less dependent on the approval of her peers.

The teen years are also a key time when we form beliefs and behaviour about our sexual desirability: am I fanciable? Do boys/girls want to date me? What do I have to do to be desirable?

Sarah: last-at-the-bar drinking buddy

Sarah, a vivacious thirty-six-year-old, came to see me because she felt she was not only sabotaging herself in an endless effort to lose weight and cut down on her drinking but, even more, was sabotaging her relationships with men through a fear of not being good enough. It seemed that her unhelpful beliefs developed in her teenage years, rather than her earlier childhood.

'I had quite a happy childhood,' Sarah explained. 'My family felt very safe and good fun. We were that kind of happy fat family, like in *The Darling Buds of May* – so as long as we stuck together, all was right with the world.' (Sarah was a master at comic self-deprecation – in order to beat anyone else to it, as she later explained.)

'But when I became a teenager, things got much harder for me. My best friend in high school was gorgeous, which didn't help at all. I got used to being her fat friend. In a way, it forced me to become fun and likeable. I comforted myself by thinking: you may not fancy me, but you'll probably think I'm a nice person.'

Remembering some of the painful details of her teenage years in our sessions, Sarah had a breakthrough insight about where her beliefs about drinking may have begun: 'At one stage, my pretty friend had a boyfriend who was a rugby player. I would go with her and hang out with all the rugby boys, and I think that's where all the serious drinking started. I couldn't be the pretty girl that they might want to go out with, so I became someone they could have a drink and a laugh with instead. I'm still always the last one at a party. With the rugby boys it was seen as a totally cool thing.'

Sarah also constantly had the undermining experience of boys paying her attention in order to get to her more fanciable friend, so that when someone really did like her, she would tend to not notice and assume that they didn't. She realised for the first time in therapy that a boy who she knew thought of her as a friend, but who she didn't dare believe had any stronger feelings, actually probably felt the same way as her. 'He'd write me letters and we'd be on the phone for hours every night, but I sabotaged the potential for a romantic relationship with him early on. I remember taking him to a disco and at one point sort of physically pushing him away, then seeing the confused look on his face. I guess I never believed he could actually be interested in me as a girl-friend.'

Sarah was very upset by this memory, but it helped her begin to shift her beliefs around herself and men, and to realise how her painful teenage experiences were constricting her life now.

COMPASSION CLAUSE: LET GO OF BLAME

It is important to gain insight and understanding into where our unhelpful beliefs and behaviour originated in a way that is compassionate and accepting to ourselves and not a source of yet more disapproval, criticism and judgment. Once we recognise these patterns, we can begin to make changes to free ourselves from ways of thinking and being that are no longer helpful to us. In Chapter Six we will see what happened when Sarah talked to her fifteen-year-old self in a compassionate and empowering way.

In the same spirit, I think it is important to try and extend compassionate curiosity and understanding to the adults in our lives who may have been involved in forming these patterns. Most parents do the best they can, given their circumstances and the way they themselves were parented. What my clients and I often discover, with some gentle digging into the past (see Chapter Five), is that their mothers and/or fathers were often under enormous stress and pressure when they were parenting their young children. It could be that they had three children under five years old, little money, no help and no disposable nappies. They were exhausted, bad tempered and harsh. Or it could be that they were lost in grief at a key bereavement – perhaps the loss of their own mother or father or a stillborn baby that has never been mentioned. Or the father was working away or having an affair, and when he was home there was terrible arguing, fighting or tension. Or maybe there was a major illness or addiction in the family. None of these events would have been the responsibility of their children – they did not cause them, nor could they fix them.

It is also important to bear in mind that many of the break-through ideas about the emotional and psychological development of children have only become widely known and accepted in the past decade or so. The popularity of television programmes such as *Supernanny* with its overriding message that parenting equals unconditional love plus clear boundaries has had a wide-reaching effect, but was not widely known to earlier generations.

DRAW YOUR FAMILY TREE

It might be interesting and helpful for you to draw your family tree at this point. This might help you to think about how you were brought up and begin to identify what personal rules and beliefs this may have given you. You could start with grandparents and work down to where you fit in. The standard is to use circles for females, squares for males, to link couples with a line and place children in a row beneath their parents, but don't worry too much about how it looks.

In therapy we call this a genogram and the idea is to enter any information that might help you gain insight into how you became who you are today – this might include life events like divorce, moving home, an affair or untimely death. You can also add psychological descriptions of people, such as critical, controlling, kind, generous – whatever you know or remember about the person. You may even want to talk to a trusted family member to find out more details. If this process brings up painful memories that feel too difficult to deal with alone, then try to talk to someone you trust or think about arranging a visit to a counsellor or therapist. (There are some useful contacts listed in the Resources section – see page 218.)

SUMMARY

Here are the core ideas we've looked at in this chapter and which we will learn how to address later on in the book.

- Aim for 'good enough'.

- Examine 'conditions of worth' and the origins and value of certain beliefs and behaviours.

- Strengthen your internal locus of evaluation.

- Let go of blame.

- Draw your family tree to help identify where personal rules and beliefs may come from.

CHAPTER THREE

The Different Shades of Lovely: Which One Are You?

When I worked as a psychologist in Holloway Prison – Europe's largest women's remand facility with over 400 inmates – part of my work there involved teaching an assertiveness-training programme (a source of some amusement to friends and colleagues as this was a key part of my own struggle). The experience taught me a valuable lesson: that very few people are assertive in all areas of their life. We all seem to have at least one weak spot and, conversely, most of us have at least one area where we do manage calm, clear, communication. Importantly, this means that effective communication is a skill that we can learn (or learn to transfer from our strongest areas), rather than something lucky people are born with and others are born without.

In the group we did an exercise called the Line Game, where an imaginary line is drawn across the room and the characters from psychologist Anne Dickson's excellent book on assertiveness (*A Woman in Your Own Right*) are placed, theoretically, along it with name labels stuck to the floor. At one end is Dulcie Doormat, who responds passively to situations and at the other is Agnes Aggressive, whose response is verbally abusive. Near Agnes is Ivy Indirect, who is what we tend to call passive aggressive, and in the middle of the line – the one we are all aiming for – is Selma Assertive. I then read out scenarios and we would all move to the point along the line that we felt most corresponded to our response to these different scenarios. What was fascinating was how we all differed and where we were similar.

Take scenario one, for example – taking faulty goods back to a shop. I would go and stand on the Dulcie Doormat spot as this was a situation I feared and avoided. The other women would mock me with good-natured taunts such as, 'Miss, you are such a wuss', as they all rushed to the Agnes Aggressive spot ('I'd f***ing tell 'em!'). But in another scenario, such as standing your ground with an undermining, critical partner, I might be nearer the assertive spot and some of them would be hovering around Dulcie Doormat, saying this was a much harder scenario for them. When it came to responding to a driver who cuts in front of the car you are driving, we all stood at Agnes Aggressive and said that in the private space of our own car we felt safe to shout and swear and maybe even make a rude hand gesture.

I have also taught a version of the Line Game to groups of

business executives (using soft toys instead of the women's names to characterise the different styles of communication – Doormat Dog and Aggressive Alligator, for example). Most of these (mainly male) executives were very experienced and confident in their roles at work, some of them in charge of hundreds of people, making important decisions all day long. And yet they felt totally powerless to say no to one of their children's wheedling demand for another bag of sweets or to a partner's unreasonable requests.

Our responses in any given relationship or situation are about confidence, and this will depend on our set of beliefs, emotions and behaviour related to that role, relationship or situation.

WHERE ARE YOU CONFIDENT?

Few of us are able to communicate calmly and clearly in all areas of life – we probably all have a bit of a Curse-of-Lovely area of vulnerability. Here are some clients' experiences to help you identify the areas that you might like to change in yourself.

Kirsty – the Lovely parent

Kirsty admitted that she had been a slightly reluctant mother. Her feelings were mixed when she discovered she was pregnant. She was excited at the new adventure, but her memories of her own childhood were not happy and she was terrified that she would become like her own mother who had been angry, volatile and abusive. Her father was away a lot, travelling with his work, so she guessed that her mother had been stressed and unhappy, alone with three small children. 'I don't like her as a person; often I hate her,' Kirsty told me. 'I only phone or visit when I absolutely have to – through guilt or duty or because my dad has put pressure on me.'

Kirsty's positive feelings about her pregnancy centred around the hope of redemption – a healing experience of being a completely different mother from her own mum. 'I think that everything I do as a mother is so my son won't feel about me as I feel about my mum. I don't want him in therapy in thirty years' time bitching about me! I want him to like and love me and to want to spend time with me.'

Kirsty's son, Max, was three when she came to therapy. She was feeling completely overwhelmed and exhausted by her life. In a bid to give Sam complete, unconditional love, she was almost completely unable to set any boundaries. She couldn't bear to hear him cry, so soothed him to sleep every night in her arms, brought him into the marital bed when he woke at night and was becoming more and more sleep deprived. She played with him all day and arranged the family timetable around his needs and desires. She described the tipping point that finally brought her to therapy:

'Whenever we go to the supermarket, I buy him a DVD from the display near the checkout. I know I shouldn't have started this because, of course, I've created an expectation in him that he will always get one. If I say, "No, not today, we've got enough DVDs", he starts to cry and if I don't give in quickly, he will throw a full-blown tantrum, shouting and screaming so that everyone looks at me, and I know they're thinking: what a terrible mother!'

But on the occasion Kirsty was telling me about, she didn't actually have enough money to buy a DVD, so had to drag the screaming Sam away, thinking she had hurt his feelings so badly that he would be damaged for life. Worse, he was very vocal in his tantrum: 'I hate you, I hate you, Mummy. I hate you!'

'I can't bear to see his pain and suffering,' she sobbed. 'And to know I have caused that is unbearable. But I can't go on like this. He is ruining my life and I feel so resentful, yet guilty that I am turning into my mother. He hates me already.' Paradoxically, Kirsty had created the very scenario she most feared.

Not all Lovely parents are the same as Kirsty, but it is quite a common pattern for mums (and many dads). You will notice that as is so often the case with Lovelies, key words or themes here are guilt, resentment and creating expectations you feel you can't break (without causing a lot of anger, which feels unbearable).

Motherhood often feeds into cultural ideals of woman-hood and can exacerbate any tendencies we already had towards self-sacrifice or martyrdom. As Susan Faludi writes in *Backlash*: 'Displays of deference and martyrdom ... are the culture's traditional badges of female honour, billed as bringing women social approval and love.' As one heavily pregnant professional client wrote to me after her first session: 'I had got sucked into this idea that I have to put my own needs last when I become a mum, otherwise I will be a bad mother. Thank you for explaining that if I don't look after myself and find ways to "fill up my tank" with fuel, then I can't give anything effectively to my child. I feel hope again!'

Amanda – the Lovely partner

Amanda felt she had finally found true love at the age of forty-five and she was ecstatically happy. Her heart had been broken by her first serious boyfriend when she was twenty-three and although she had had many romances, dates and flings, she had not really trusted men since then.

'The guys always seem to hold all the cards,' Amanda told me, as she explained why she was seeking therapy. 'You never really know what they are thinking and they always seem to have some back-up date in the background. But I want this to be different.'

Amanda had met Simon and wanted to move forward into the kind of happy-ever-after promised by the movies. But as we all know, life is rarely that straightforward. Simon had been through a bitter divorce, which had left him bruised and fragile, and with a teenage son who lived with him every week-end in a small town several hundred miles from where Amanda was based. But she threw herself into the relationship with an amazing generosity of spirit, money, time and energy. She learnt to play 'Call of Duty' on the computer, so she could shoot virtual aliens and bond with the unwelcoming son, she put up with his mess in the bathroom, picking through the soggy towels to find one dry enough to use and silently threw away empty pizza boxes left lying around in the kitchen.

Amanda did everything she thought the perfect girlfriend should do – cooking, cleaning, ironing – even though Simon didn't actually ask her to do any of these things. She suffered the long train journey to visit him every weekend, beginning to hate the inevitable Sunday afternoon rail-replacement buses and the loss of personal weekend catch-up time. They usually talked on the phone for two hours every night, Amanda often finding herself sympathising with his complicated work and family problems, but minimising her own issues and struggles.

Then Amanda's health began to suffer. She developed stomach pains to the point where she went to her GP because she thought she may have stomach cancer. 'Can you remember when the stomach pains started?' I asked. 'Did it link with anything?' She thought for a moment. 'I had just got on the train from his station …' she said. 'Do you remember what you were feeling?' I asked her. 'I was simmering with resentment. I felt like I had swallowed so much …' 'Into your stomach?' 'Yes! My goodness – that is it, that is the stomach pain. In fact, I've been feeling it in my throat too. I'm not ill – I'm sick with resentment!'

Together we designed something called the Resentment Barometer: what is the reading? What do I need? What is stopping me asking for it? What is the fear? Amanda identified that the fear was of losing his love: 'If I ask for what I need, he will withdraw his love,' she reasoned. She uncovered other

Rigid Personal Rules: I MUST NOT MAKE A FUSS, I MUST NOT BE A BURDEN.

This was the beginning of insight and understanding for Amanda, but as we all know, change is by far the slowest and hardest part. We will catch up with her again in Chapter Four.

The Lovely partner is not just found in the courtship phase, where we are often trying to be 'at our best' to win and keep the guy or girl. You may recognise yourself in your marriage or long-term relationship as the one who seems to give too much, to do all the compromising or 'emotional smoothing'. And it feels too risky, too exposing and scary to say any of this and identify and ask for what you really want, which may vary from the practical ('I need you to help with the laundry') to the (far more scary) emotional ('I need more love and attention from you'). And this can apply to men as well as women, gay couples as well as straight.

Often, Lovelies are subconsciously attracted to people who have little problem with the areas in which they themselves struggle (Harville Hendrix gives a very clear explanation of this phenomenon in his book: *Getting the Love you Want*). For example, as Lovelies we end up in a relationship with someone who is comfortable with their own and other people's anger, and we delegate to them all the assertive communication work in the relationship (saying no to people, getting a refund, dealing with the builder, etc.). But this allocation of roles – where our partner takes on the confrontations, while we are in charge of the Lovely behaviours – can backfire, leaving us feeling intimidated, trapped and resentful.

Hamish – the Lovely man

I'm including the case of Hamish here to illustrate that the
Curse of Lovely is not just something that afflicts women. As
I mentioned earlier, I have had several male clients who have
responded enthusiastically to the concept and feel just as trapped
by the expectations of others as do the super-nice women who
struggle to express the suppressed sides of themselves.

I already had a strong feeling that Hamish would have this
problem when the receptionist who took his booking gushed:
'He seems a lovely man.' Whenever anyone describes a person
as 'lovely', my suspicion is alerted. I wonder: at what cost to
them does that adjective come?

I soon found out the cost for Hamish. He had a lovely,
charming, charismatic smile, and was instantly warm and
engaging, cracking jokes, making me laugh. He worked in IT
and helped *everyone* with their computer problems, even
though that wasn't actually his job. Everyone loved Hamish!
And guess what? Beneath his smiling, helpful exterior Hamish
burned with resentment: 'I feel incredibly caged in all aspects
of my life,' he admitted. 'Everyone thinks I am this nice guy –
and of course, part of me is and I like that part of me. But I
also have this dark side that bubbles underneath, mocking me
and those around me.'

Hamish fought constantly to keep what he viewed as his
dark, unacceptable side, completely out of sight of others,
which took a huge amount of effort and can never be a 100
per cent effective strategy for anyone. 'Occasionally, a seemingly trivial thing will cause me to explode, and then people

seem to recoil away from me in shock and disappointment. I don't shout and scream – it's more that I radiate ice-cold anger or fire cruel arrows of sarcasm at them.' 'What happens then?' I asked. 'Well, I feel so embarrassed that I am then super-super-nice to try and make amends.'

I often ask clients to draw a picture of what qualities they see themselves portraying to other people and what they hold down inside, or suppress (you can do this exercise on page 54). When Hamish drew his picture he drew beams of saintly light around his body and wrote around them: 'Can't say no', 'Looks after everyone' and 'Keeps all the plates spinning'. Inside his body he drew dark swirls and wrote: 'My dad'. Hamish's dad walked out on his mum and their two small children when Hamish was four years old. 'He is a cold and ruthless man,' said Hamish. 'And I am terrified that I am like him. We are both very stubborn,' he laughed, darkly.

Hamish's Lovely pattern also caused conflict with his wife. In trying so hard to be unlike his father, he denied much of his masculine side; he was super-nice and in touch with his feminine side, but suppressed so much that his wife said he was secretive and accused him of having affairs (especially as she had seen how all the girls at work responded so enthusiastically to his Loveliness, which only fed her suspicions, of course).

So Hamish's task was to see if he could integrate the two sides of himself. Could he retain enough of the 'nice guy' that he and others liked and appreciated, while allowing enough of his 'dark' side out so that it didn't reach the point at which it exploded? We will see how Hamish got on with this in Chapter Four.

Jessica – the Lovely colleague

When Jessica first came to see me she was very excited by the idea of the Curse of Lovely. 'That is completely me!' she cried. She felt she had no life outside of a 'dead-end job' where she worked long hours of unpaid overtime, doing the work of two people but with no recognition or support and, inevitably, feeling very stressed. She wanted to lose weight, make friends, sort out her relationship and enjoy everything the city had to offer, but felt drained, depressed and exhausted after every working day. 'Nothing is going right. I feel like a five-year-old waiting for someone to tell me what to do in my life.' And she started crying – gently, but with a heart-wrenching helplessness.

Five was a key age for Jessica. Her parents split up when she was one, and her mother took her to live with her parents (Jessica's maternal grandparents), so they could look after her while her mother went out to work to support the household. By five, she can remember being a very good little girl and desperate for the approval of her very strict grandfather who looked after her every day after school and believed that children should be seen and not heard. He had a volatile temper, but as long as she obeyed the rules, did as she was told, worked hard and kept quiet, Jessica felt safe and secure.

Fast-forward twenty-five years, however, and Jessica is still living her life governed by her five-year-old's Rigid Personal Rules. The very same rules that were quite effective in getting her needs met then are now causing her to feel miserable, exploited and helpless, as she does as she's told, works hard and keeps quiet. 'I need to be able to stand up for myself, say no to all that extra work they pile on to me and go home on time.' Jessica smiled a lovely smile, adding, 'But that is about as likely as me wearing size eight jeans!'

Together we drew a picture of how Jessica felt she looked to others – an ever-smiling, ever-willing angel – and we talked about the idea of experimenting with being just 1 per cent less lovely. What might that mean in practice, I asked? Could she think of something she could do tomorrow which would represent that 1 per cent? 'Maybe say no when a colleague asks you to help them do a spreadsheet?' Jessica looked worried and shook her head. 'What is the fear?' I asked. 'Does an image come up for you?' 'My fear is that if I was even 1 per cent less Lovely, then I would be a tantruming five-year-old who would be sacked in five minutes flat!'

These are the kinds of fears and images that keep many of us trapped in rigid rules and behaviour for decades. It is only when we dare to begin experimenting with doing something different that we can start to break the Curse.

Jessica continued in therapy for six months and became a very brave experimenter, going way beyond the 1 per cent I initially suggested. We will look at how she managed to achieve this in Chapters Seven and Eight.

Liz – the Lovely friend

Forty-five-year-old Liz travelled hundreds of miles for a two-hour therapy session. She sat down with a sigh: 'On the train today I actually thought that this session is my version of going to a spa. I can't remember the last time I did something purely for myself.'

Since her divorce five years earlier Liz said she had felt 'oppressed by responsibility'. She worked exceptionally hard as the CEO of an arts centre, worried about supporting her two teenagers emotionally and financially and kept up with a large circle of friends. 'I've never liked to upset anyone or let them down, but now it's got to the point where I'm over-whelmed by commitments and feel I'm out of touch with what I want and even with what I really feel.'

I pointed out that Liz looked a bit like a naughty schoolgirl when she mentioned the idea of having time for herself, and I wondered what she was thinking. She smiled sheepishly: 'I'm thinking, who's going to tell me off?'

Together we worked out that one of the reasons she strug-gled to say no to anything and set reasonable limits (especially with friends) was a childhood link between doing what you want to do and being unlikeable, a message that came from her disapproving father. 'Three years ago he told me, "I always regret that I ever allowed you to go to that university because you came back with pink hair and your own opinions." I want to say to him, "You don't have to dislike me, just because I'm doing my own thing."' But the legacy of this was a belief that to be likeable she must do what she thinks others want, and Rigid Personal Rules which included I MUST NEVER LET ANYONE DOWN.

I asked Liz if she could experiment with letting friends down. Starting in a small, safe way, was there anything she could cancel that she didn't really want to do, and see how she survived the outcome? She said that she had agreed to go to a friend's event that night to support her, but really she would like to have a soak in the bath and an early night. She promised to cancel and see how she felt. She also agreed to keep a notebook logging this and other behavioural experiments. We will see how she got on with this in Chapter Nine.

Many Lovelies struggle to say no and set boundaries with friends, neighbours, colleagues and acquaintances. Be it agreeing to go to their events, taking their phone calls at inconvenient moments or being an ever-available shoulder to cry on, it is often about putting others' needs before your own and not feeling you have the right to say no.

The Lovely professionals

As we know, Lovelies have a tendency towards 'all-or-nothing' thinking: if I am not totally 100 per cent one thing, then I am the other (bad) thing. This often translates as: if I am not completely compassionate, giving people what they want, then I am a mean, selfish, bad (add your own appropriate negative word here) person. This can lead to burnout and what is called 'compassion fatigue'. If you believe you are *only* a good person if you try to help the world's needy and say yes to everyone's requests and desires, then you will, inevitably, become overwhelmed, resentful and burnt out.

I'm guessing that many people reading this book might work in the so-called 'caring' professions, as I think this is a natural calling for Lovelies. But like the proverbial moth to a flame, it is a bright light that ends up burning many decent, well-meaning people.

You may recognise yourself in some or all of the scenarios above, but the important thing to remember is that the beliefs and behaviours that underpin them are learnt and can, therefore, be relearnt in ways that will support your health and happiness.

We will shortly look at ways for you to break the Curse and get back in touch with your needs, but first, you might like to take a moment to do the exercise below and uncover your own unique shades of Lovely.

The Curse of Lovely picture exercise

This is the exercise I asked Hamish and Jessica to do. It is something I often do with clients at the beginning of our work together. It is quite playful, so brings a bit of lightness to what can feel a weighed-down, heavy 'stuckness'. I've included my picture opposite to help you understand how to create your own.

In a dedicated notebook if you are using one or on a piece of paper, draw a simple picture of a figure that represents you. It helps if the figure is wearing a triangular gown, so that there is space for you to write in it, but otherwise, straight-line 'stick' arms and legs and a simple circle for a head, is fine. I always put a big smile on the face, because most Lovelies tend to smile a lot. Customising with some squiggles for hair that looks like your own is another detail I enjoy.

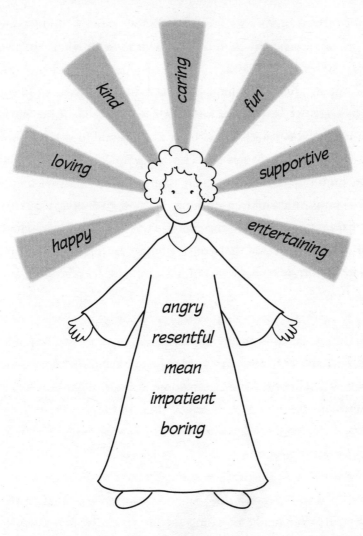

Next, draw some lines radiating out from the head and body – a bit like those in religious images of the Madonna or saints – leaving enough space so you can write next to or in them. You can put arrow heads on them too if you like (pointing away from 'you'), as they represent the ways in which you give energy out to people and the world.

The next step is to write words or phrases along these lines or arrows that capture your own sense of what you give out, or *radiate* to others. These can be *behaviours* – for example, always smiling, always ready to listen, time for everyone, never say no, make others laugh, keep the party going ... The list is endless, but very personal to you. Or they could be personal rules that you communicate to others such as: I am open all hours, I will always put my partner first, I will refuse my children nothing. Write the ideas down fairly quickly without giving the exercise too much thought. These are the parts of you that you are happy for others to see and that are often very positive things, but can feel draining and endless.

Now think about what you do *not* easily (or ever) express to others. What is pushed down inside, unexpressed and simmering away? Inside your picture (inside the triangular gown, if you drew one) write down some ideas of what you feel is bubbling away here. Is it anger? Is it sadness? Resentment? What about me? Just write a few things – those that feel most powerful to you.

Now look at the picture. You don't have to do anything else for the time being, but this will give you a strong visual awareness of what might be going on for you in your particular shade of the Curse of Lovely – remembering that everyone differs in respect to the situations and relationships where they feel able to communicate assertively.

SUMMARY

In this chapter we've got a little closer to finding out what the Curse of Lovely actually means to us and where we are as a result:

- Where would you be on the Line Game? Think about which relationships and situations you are most – and least – confident in.

- Check your Resentment Barometer.

- Beware of all-or-nothing thinking.

- Try the picture exercise to give yourself a visual representation of what might be going on for you in your own shade of the Curse of Lovely.

CHAPTER FOUR

Tune In – What is Your Body Telling You?

Think back to the last chapter and the drawing exercise you have just completed – or maybe just envisaged. What did you write on the inside of the figure; what are your suppressed emotions? (Common responses are: anger, resentment, unkindness, disinterest, selfishness, fear, cruelty, rage ...) You have tuned in enough to know what you hide from the world and push inside – that which simmers underneath.

Your next challenge is to tune in *regularly* to your body to begin to identify *when* and *how* your feelings manifest themselves physically and how this links to what you are thinking (thoughts) and what you do (behaviour).

When I first mention this to clients, no one really knows

what I am talking about, as the concept seems too vague. But I had a strong sense, starting with my own experience, that part of the Curse of Lovely is about overriding the messages we constantly receive from our bodies, and if we can begin to tune in to these messages, we can start to break the Curse. Initially, we hear them, but ignore them; then it can become such an ingrained habit that we don't even hear them any more, or they are like little ghostly voices, whispering to us in the wind.

In this chapter I want you to get used to listening to your body and hearing what it has to say. Your truth, we could call it. I don't expect, at this point, for you to try and change anything; but by reading the next few chapters with an open mind you will help to prepare yourself as fully as possible to try and do something different.

CHECK IN TO YOUR BODY

Take the example that I opened the book with – my broken arm. In the ten days between falling over at the barn dance and finally getting an x-ray at the hospital I received so many messages from my body. First there was the pain – sharp if I moved my arm too far, but often just dull and throbbing. Sometimes I felt vaguely nauseous, but didn't know why. My nights became very disturbed as I couldn't find a comfortable position, or, if I did, the pain woke me up if I turned in my sleep. So I became very sleep deprived and irritable. But I didn't listen to what any of these – quite loud – messages were trying to tell me.

Now obviously this is quite an extreme example, but I think we are all constantly receiving important information from our bodies, most of which we ignore or can't even hear any more. It is like a radio that is broadcasting on a frequency too obscure for our receivers to pick up. Many of my clients live their lives from the neck upwards – often amazingly analytical, intelligent and thoughtful, yet totally cut off from what their bodies are telling them.

Are you breathing right now? Yes, I know, of course you are. But just take a moment to *notice* your breathing. Are you sitting at a desk, working on a computer? I recently read that many of us unconsciously hold our breath, or breathe shallowly, while responding to emails. Is yours high in your chest or is your stomach rising and falling with the in and the out breaths? Are you holding your breath, even slightly? Now do a quick scan of the rest of your body, starting with your toes and mentally moving all the way up to the top of your head. What can you identify? Where do you feel heat, coolness, stiffness, aching? Are you hungry, thirsty, in pain, in need of the toilet or some fresh air? What are you ignoring or overriding in your body at this moment? Starting to listen to these messages is one of the ways back to choice and well-being.

In Chapter Ten, you'll find a breathing exercise you can do but for now you may just want to familiarise yourself with what your body is trying to tell you.

Jessica and the need to pee

Jessica the Lovely colleague who wanted to be more assertive at work and in life (see page 50) knew exactly what I was talking about when I mentioned listening to her body: 'Is it like when you are with a group of people and you need to go to the toilet, but you daren't say anything or get up because you don't want to interrupt the conversation or draw attention to yourself?' 'That is a great example,' I said. 'Do you do that?' She looked amazed, then embarrassed: 'I think I do it the whole time; that is the complete norm for me.'

Now be honest, how many of you are nodding your heads in agreement? Since that conversation with Jessica, I have asked a lot of people the same question and it is fascinating how many admit that they often ignore their body's message that they need to go to the toilet, especially when they are with other people. They also admit that they sometimes – or often – override their body telling them they are thirsty, hungry, tired or stressed. But why, you might be asking yourself, does this matter?

You may have come across the idea of 'listening to your body' in a medical or exercise context. Often, a yoga or fitness instructor will tell you to listen to your body, so that you don't over-exert yourself and damage a muscle or ligament. But tuning into your bodily sensations can also help you tune in to and identify your emotions. People struggle to recognise and name their feelings; it is not something we are generally taught to do at school or home. But they are very physically based (hence 'feel'-ings) and if you can begin to identify the bodily sensation, then you can also name it as an emotion. This, in turn, will help you to explore what the emotions might *mean* and how they are linked to your thoughts and behaviour.

Possibly one of the easiest emotions to identify is anxiety. This is a fear response to a perceived threat in the environment, even if this perceived 'threat' is actually a *thought* (such as a memory) in our minds. This is governed by our primitive fight, flight or freeze response (the body's physiological reaction to a perceived threat). Here is how Monika identified how her anxiety linked with her thoughts and behaviour.

Tune in with your body

Check in with your body a few times a day. A good idea is to stick a coloured adhesive dot on to things you use regularly – for example, the kettle, your computer, the bathroom mirror. Then whenever you see one, take a deep breath and take your attention to your body.

Where is there tension, pain, tightness? Where is there warmth, coldness, dryness, itchiness? What do you notice and how does it relate to any emotions you can identify? All of this is really helpful information as you will begin to become more aware of what is going on in your body that you may have – up until now – ignored.

Monika feels the fear

Monika, the 1000-watt light bulb (see page 24) had to go away on a week-long residential course for work. She arrived at the beautiful stately home in the countryside feeling quite excited: a week away from routine with all meals cooked – how bad can that be? The first evening she sat down at the large dining table joining in the chat and enjoying the delicious homemade food. She felt a bit buzzy and decided to take a moment to check in with her body. She noticed that her heart was racing and her mouth was dry. She also realised that she had been drinking glass after glass of water, filling it up time and again from the jug.

That night, as she lay in bed, Monika reflected on her behaviour. At home she hardly ever drank water with her dinner, and certainly not five or six glasses.

Suddenly, a vivid image came to her. She was sitting at the family supper table with her mum, dad and brother. She would refill her water glass so often that her dad used to joke that he should install a hosepipe directly to the table for her. Her mum would look sour and go and refill the jug, despite Monika's protestations that she could do it. It was very tense. Her mum was often angry with her dad. She was bitter and resentful that she did so much to look after their family and her dad coped with this by making jokes, which Monika, his favourite, laughed at loudly which seemed to make her mum even more angry. Caught in the middle of them, Monika remembered endlessly refilling her water glass – probably as an anxious dis-placement activity, she now realised.

It was suddenly crystal clear: sitting at the dining table among unknown people had subconsciously taken Monika back to the tension of her childhood meals. She had felt anxious at the table and had responded by drinking lots of water, laughing very loudly at people's jokes and waving her arms about – all of which she remembered doing as a child (often knocking things over as a result which, of course, added to the tension and anxiety).

Monika decided not to do anything drastically different, but to keep tuning in and remembering to breathe more slowly when she felt her heart racing. She realised that her reaction felt very similar to what she would find herself doing at a larger social gathering. The fear of any slight sign of disapproval or tension would switch on her 1000-watt light bulb and she would be anxiously over-performing and radiating energy before she even realised what had happened.

The physical manifestations of anxiety are close cousins of those of anger. *Star Wars* sage Yoda was not far wrong when he said that 'fear turns to anger'.

Hamish feels the anger

Hamish the Lovely man (see page 48) felt growing resentment that his wife always left the empty porridge saucepan unwashed on the kitchen counter. For months Hamish had silently and dutifully washed out the pan – the hard and congealed dollops stuck to the sides, sticky and resistant to his efforts with the scourer. Inside his body he was *seething* with unacknowledged rage and resentment, but without first recognising this, he couldn't begin to think about his options for action. Instead, the anger would seep out at other times, unexpectedly. So, for example, he might find himself snapping with inappropriate force when his wife suggested they watch *MasterChef* on TV: 'I don't know why you like that; it's vacuous rubbish!' he'd snipe, much to her amazement. Or he would snarl abuse at other drivers on his way to work. (Interestingly, I have found this to be a classic Lovely outlet for unacknowledged anger that feels safe and anonymous; until someone stops their car and comes over to take you up on it, that is.)

Every week I urged Hamish to try and notice what happened in his body at various times. Often, I would say to him in the session: 'What are you feeling in your body now, at this moment? Where is it?' This was really hard for him, as it is for many of us, especially if we were brought up to believe that certain powerful (or *all*) emotions are bad or wrong and we learnt to push them down ('suppress' them) as a result, until we no longer notice them. But they are, of course, still there, and will come out or affect our bodies in one way or another.

One week Hamish came to his session and announced that he had had a light-bulb moment. 'I had a disagreement with my wife,' he told me. 'And I could feel a surge of adrenalin in my body.' 'That is brilliant,' I said (obviously *not* referring to the argument). 'Well done for noticing. What exactly did the adrenalin surge feel like? What was happening?' 'Well, I felt quite jittery, and when I looked at my hands, they were shaking slightly. I just wanted to get out of the room as quickly as possible before I said something awful, but my wife kept firing questions at me. I thought, if I open my mouth, it will all be over; there will be no going back. But my wife stormed off first, crying and screaming that I was a cold-hearted bastard and my face looked like a blank mask.'

As Hamish began to get more tuned in to what was going on in his body, he became more curious about how the sensations were made better or worse depending on what thoughts he attached to them. When he judged himself harshly with thoughts like 'You are turning into Pa! You are evil and cold-hearted. Maria will find out and leave you', the stress was unbearable and he could feel himself freezing ('like a rabbit in the grass'). This made Maria even angrier as she felt him emotionally withdraw. But when he could calmly voice to himself – and, finally, to his wife – his fear that he was turning into his father, she was then able to reassure him and it brought them closer together.

We will look more closely at the effects of our thoughts (especially our internal critical dialogue) on our emotions and behaviour in the next chapter.

NOTES ON ANGER

A friend who heard I was writing this book sent me an email: 'Can you address the fear we feel ourselves at the extent of our own anger ... I get scared by the power of my own anger and the effect it has on other people ... and, invariably, that leads "post outburst" to a form of shock at my own capacity to "explode like that", then total wretchedness at the effect of the fallout of my anger.'

As I mentioned much earlier, a classic Lovely pattern is to suppress *any* feelings of anger for fear of getting into conflict with others. But this is, of course, ultimately unsustainable and the anger will out in a seemingly uncontrollable way – scaring and shocking both to ourselves and others. The emotional 'Resentment Barometer' that Amanda designed for use with her partner and his son (see page 45) can be used by all of us. It gives us a chance to identify feelings on the mild end of the anger range (for example, annoyance, disappointment, hurt) and recognise our choices to do something different before the feelings build into inappropriate rage and explosion as described above. The Lovely person may have felt so traumatised by their very rare explosion of anger that they fight to never let this happen again, concealing in the process all angry feelings from everyone, even themselves (as Hamish had done). They therefore gain little or no experience in how to handle difficult people, situations and conversations.

We need practice so that we learn that we do have the skills to handle these things and that our catastrophically fearful predictions are unlikely to be true (see Chapters Seven and Eight for skills and behavioural experiments).

One of my clients gave me a more visual metaphor for her anger, describing it as the hot apple filling bubbling away in the oven beneath the lovely crumble topping. She had to monitor the heat of the filling to make sure it didn't bubble over the topping and ruin the dessert. She would take action as necessary, such as taking it out of the oven (i.e. removing herself from the source of 'heat'/annoyance) or saying something, calmly, to the source.

WHAT ARE YOU NOT SAYING?

The next step for Hamish was to begin to notice what he was *not* saying to his wife or to the people at work who made him feel angry as well. This 'editing out', as I call it, is really helpful information to investigate, where we look at the thoughts – especially old rules and beliefs – that are powering our emotional reactions and our behaviour.

See if you can try to monitor what you go to great lengths *not* to say to the people in your life. You can just observe that monologue in your head or you could try and write it down, say in your notebook last thing at night. Writing tends to give more power to our insights, but do what you are most comfortable with. Here are some examples of clients observing and monitoring what they are editing out.

Ella edits out her real self

Because of her traumatic teenage experience of feeling ridiculed, rejected and excluded (see page 33) friendship exerted a powerful pull in Ella's life. She put superhuman effort into maintaining a vast social circle, but was always paranoid that people were talking about her behind her back and excluding her from events. 'I'm no one's best friend,' she would sigh. 'When it comes to their weddings and christenings, I am never asked to be the bridesmaid or godmother; I'm always last choice ... '

One day I asked Ella to try to monitor for a whole week what she was thinking, but not saying when with her friends. The results were very revealing. Ella realised that she edited out almost everything that made her feel different from the person who was speaking. So if they said they loved a film or TV series, Ella would nod in agreement, even if she thought the total opposite. When one girl was moaning about her lack of money and how she would love to be able to afford to go to a spa, Ella sympathised but omitted to mention that she had been to a spa that very weekend! She even realised that she was carrying a bag with the spa's branding on it, and began to think about how she could hide it or invent a story as to why she was carrying it. 'Later, as I wrote all this up in my journal, I began to see the funny side,' she said. 'I thought, if this was a cartoon, I would be stuffing the bag into my mouth, trying to eat it to destroy the evidence!'

Ella's close monitoring of her editing enabled her to see that her teen beliefs were still totally controlling her behaviour: as long as she could keep her real self under the radar, she would fit in and be part of the 'cool' crowd who had access to all the parties and boy action. Only now they were all in their early thirties, this didn't really work. Instead, Ella felt isolated and not deeply connected to anyone because she never dared to reveal her true thoughts and feelings.

We'll catch up with Ella again in Chapter Eight to see how she experimented with slowly changing this.

I don't really like the word 'collude' because I feel it is a negative, critical word and, as you may have noticed, I try and avoid judgmental language. But I couldn't really think of a word to describe more accurately what it is we do when we don't dare to voice our disagreement with someone we disagree with. It's that fear-of-conflict thing again: why risk anger and discord, when you can ignore what you are really thinking and have harmony? But this comes at a price to ourselves. Again, we are not daring to reveal who we really are – our values, beliefs, tastes and opinions – so the other person can never really know who we are either. The relationship suffers because it is not very authentic. And our sense of self-worth suffers because we don't trust that they like us for who we are – they may only like us because we agree with them.

I am not saying you should immediately start to speak the truth, the whole truth and nothing but the truth; don't let me give you a new *should* to add to your list of perfectionist challenges (see Chapter Five). No, I would just encourage you for now to begin *noticing* what the true responses are inside your head before acting on them – that is something we'll come to later. Kirsty the Lovely parent (see page 42) gave me a good example.

Kirsty edits out her real feelings

Kirsty's mother came round for tea one day and after observing that the house wasn't very tidy, Max wasn't properly toilet trained and the tea wasn't leaf, she launched into a nasty tirade about Kirsty's sister-in-law Angela. The monologue inside

Kirsty's head ran something like this: 'God, you are such a mean old woman. You are so jealous of Angela because she has married your precious son and is not the woman you would have picked for him. I actually like her; she is the best thing that ever happened to him, and I will not listen to you slagging her off like that.' What Kirsty actually did, however, was smile weakly at the bitchy jibes, protest mildly at the meanest of the comments ('Oh Mum, I think she does her best with the kids') and try to suggest alternative viewpoints, but with little force in her tone, volume or body language.

I am not criticising Kirsty in any way. Her inner child is very powerfully activated in the presence of her mother, so to even speak one tiny part of her thoughts is incredibly brave and high up her hierarchy of fear (which we will look at in Chapter Eight). And to notice her internal, disagreeing monologue is also a fantastic first step, as awareness almost invariably leads to change, but in its own sweet time.

Amanda edits out her real desires

We met Amanda the Lovely partner in Chapter Three. She had begun to tune in to her what her body was trying to tell her through stomach problems which she'd realised were linked to her unexpressed anger – the idea that she was 'swallowing' her resentment and it was burning her throat and stomach.

She began to monitor what we named her Resentment Barometer, observing her body whenever she agreed to things she didn't want to do, offered to do things (ironing, cooking) she didn't want to do or let that nightly phone call go on for two hours when she wanted to snuggle up in bed with a mug of hot chocolate and watch telly.

I asked her to try and notice, then later write down, the words in her head that she wasn't saying. She soon had some clear examples of what she was editing out. For example, to the teenage son: 'Please put the wet towels away in the airing cupboard', 'I don't want to play Call of Duty tonight', 'I would like some time alone with your dad' and 'I find it offensive the way you talk about girls; please don't do that in front of me'. What she didn't say to her boyfriend included: 'Can I call you back later when *The Killing* is over?', 'I'm going to take some time for myself this weekend – I will visit you next weekend' and 'I don't want to be patted on the shoulder at 11pm for sex, thank you very much; a woman needs foreplay and seduction.'

Often, clients will give voice to what they *really* want to say to their partners once in the safety of my consulting room. Such venom seems to come out of the sweetest of mouths. 'Shall we think of a safe way you could say some of this to your partner?' I ask. This is usually met with a sharp intake of breath and a vigorous shake of the head. 'God, no. I couldn't begin to say any of this to him/her.' 'Why not? What is your fear?' I ask. They usually look totally horrified: 'They would be out of the door in a second' (or variations on that theme). It seems that the fear of losing their partner and/or their partner's love is what keeps them mute – mute, but simmering with resentment and anger which, as I always say, will be seeping out like poisonous gas, definitely registered – on some level – by their partners.

We will look at ways to bravely, but safely, speak the unspeakable in Chapters Eight and Nine, but let's look here at just *why* it is that we edit out what we really want to say? There are many and complex reasons, but they probably come down to a combination of the two prime motivators identified in Chapter Two: anger avoidance and approval seeking. Kirsty was both trying to avoid her mother's disapproval and displeasure and make her be more pleasant and approving. Amanda was doing everything she thought necessary to win and keep her partner's love and approval. But sometimes there are certain people in our life who leave us feeling that we do not have the right to feel and express our emotions, especially if these emotions are negative.

THE AUCTION OF MISERIES

One of my first ever clients, Adrianna, came up with the wonderful phrase, the Auction of Miseries, in honour of the author Anton Chekhov, who weighed the sum of human misery in his brilliant but bleak depictions of late nineteenth-century Russian life.

When I first met Adrianna her life was incredibly hard. She was struggling to survive as a single working mother in a foreign country with no support from her family or the father of her child. In addition, her best friend from childhood – one of her most important relationships – still demanded support (both financial and emotional) from her, yet failed to even listen to her in her hour of need. This caused her enormous pain and hurt. When Adrianna tearfully recounted their conversations, it seemed to me that the friend would always 'trump' Adrianna's struggles with her own problems: 'Ah yes, but at least you have a mother – mine is dead' or 'But at least you have a child; I will never meet a man.'

Non-Lovelies will often shake their heads in bafflement at these dynamics: why on earth do we still give these so-called friends the time of day? Get rid of them and find new ones, they tell us with bossy certainty. But of course, it is not that easy. The Lovely, on some level, often *believes* the Auction-of-Misery friend that because they are 'luckier' than them, they must feel guilty and pay for this with a one-way friendship involving endless sympathy, listening and support in order, somehow, to (usually subconsciously) make it all better for the friend.

If you think back to your childhood, this response is often historically underpinned with a set of rules and beliefs that formed back then in relation to key adults in your life. The belief may go something like this: if I make this person happier, then they will be nice to me.

What really helped Adrianna was telling her that I believe that there is no hierarchy of emotional pain. Well-meaning people will often try to cheer you up by reminding you of the good things you still have in your life ('well, at least you've still got a job/home/marriage/both your legs …') or ask you to think of the starving children in Africa or victims of the latest natural disaster and realise how well off you are; but this only serves to shame you into feeling you are not allowed your own unhappiness and that it has no relative value in a supposed hierarchy of pain. For a Lovely, this often fits in with your deep-seated belief (usually from childhood) that you yourself have little worth, so you accept that your pain has less value than other people's. Adrianna found this idea really freeing, and it allowed her to feel more entitled to stand up to her manipulative friend (and pursue the father of her child for financial support).

Together, we updated her metaphor: she didn't choose to bid in the Auction of Miseries, but withdrew her lot to work on it privately, and refused to feel guilty about her friend's lot.

DO YOU EDIT OUT THE TRUTH, THEN OVER-GIVE?

The process goes like this: we think an honest thought about a person, but edit it out. We then immediately feel mean, guilty and ashamed that we have had the thought. We then over-compensate by offering something Lovely – either an actual suggestion to do something we know we don't want to do ('Let's have dinner!' or 'Why don't you come and stay!' or 'Why don't I help you with that?') or Lovely words that are slightly dishonest ('Oh, you poor thing, that sounds terrible' or 'Yes, how dare they do that to you?').

Rebecca, whose story you will read later (see page 202), came up with a very visual metaphor for how this felt to her: 'It's like I have a Lovely vomit problem!' she said. 'Things just seem to come out of my mouth like I have no control over them. By the time I realise, it is too late to stop the words. I offer things without really thinking if I want to do them. I usually almost immediately realise that I don't – but it's too late by then to take it back.'

I think a lot of us will identify with Rebecca's metaphor. It helps bring lightness, rather than shame, to an ingrained habit that we are trying to break. But what can we do to stop our mouths from having a life of their own? We need a pause, a gap, some small space that allows us to access our rational thinking capacity. One of the best ways to do this is to bring your attention to your breath as I outlined on page 60 – or do the breathing exercise on page 183). This will allow your thinking capacity to come through – this is the part that would tell Rebecca, for example: 'Don't invite your flatmate to the park. You want to be alone, you will regret it as soon as you say it ...'

SUMMARY

We've now seen how by tuning in regularly to our bodies we can begin to identify any physical manifestations of our feelings and how these relate to what we are thinking and doing.

- Begin to stop overriding your body's messages.

- Check in with your body using the exercise on page 60.

- Look at what you are 'editing out'. As you begin to identify what you *don't* want (to do or say), can you then begin to highlight what you *do* want?

CHAPTER FIVE

Uncover Your Ancient Rules and Beliefs

What are the personal beliefs and rules behind whatever you may have tuned in to in the last chapter? Why do we override or edit out those physical sensations, feelings and words which we are now beginning to know are there? What messages are telling us that we must not notice or act upon them? Messages about ourselves, perhaps? For example, 'I must always be polite' or 'I must always go with the flow' or maybe 'I must never cause a fuss/conflict/disagreement'. And what is the *fear* that lurks behind each thought and action?

IMAGINE YOURSELF ON AN ARCHAEOLOGICAL DIG

Imagine you are an archaeologist on an important historical dig. If you like, you could be starring in one of those old movies involving various characters in their khaki jodhpurs and pith helmets, all racing to find the hidden treasures or scrolls. The part I want you to think of is the uncovering of the precious historical objects that will throw light on to the society of the time and its legacy to us today. At first, you are digging through layers of earth very carefully with a special trowel. Then, when you hit anything at all that might be important, you switch to using a little soft brush to gently remove the dirt and dust that cling to the object, until you can finally lift it out into the light and life of the present day and begin the process of trying to analyse and understand it.

But as we know from films like the Indiana Jones series, there are always numerous obstacles to surmount before the hero can get to the ancient treasure. The most challenging of these is usually the villains whose job it is to keep Indiana away from his goal by any means possible. They are invariably armed to the teeth and know no mercy as they attack with guns, arrows, fire and poison.

Critical thoughts – the vicious guardians of the ancient scrolls

Our personal equivalents of the villains in the movies are the critical thoughts that whirl around endlessly inside our heads.

This internal critical dialogue is like the vicious guardians of the ancient scrolls, watching – in our case – over the rules and beliefs contained in what we have begun to unearth. If we try to question an old rule for living or a belief about who we are or how we should behave, then these armed thugs will point their guns, arrows and flamethrowers and threaten and scare us back into line. We feel outnumbered and overwhelmed, but, like Indiana Jones leaping to safety, we too can find creative, unexpected ways to stand up to these internal bullies.

Whose voice is saying that to you?

Our critical thoughts are so familiar to us that we may have never paused to ask who they actually belong to. This may seem an odd thing to say because we think of them as part of ourselves, but if we listen carefully, we will probably find that they have an accent, tone or phrasing that is different from the way we usually speak. This is because, generally, the critical thoughts come from significant people in our past. And although they may be very much alive and large in our lives today, it was on our childhood and adolescent brain that they had the most impact. So who is saying: 'You are so stupid – you'll never get this right!' or 'You are so selfish – help that person out!' or 'You are a loser – you will never get a boyfriend/promotion/happiness!' (I have purposely used exclamation marks because I think these voices are often shrill – perhaps like a teacher's when they were shouting over the class to be heard.)

It really helps to make a note of what your critical voices

tend to say, then you can read what you've written in a calm moment and see if you can identify who used to say those things to you. One of my clients realised she was hearing the Hungarian accent of her critical grandmother; another her long-term ice-skating coach. Of course, many of these voices belong to parents. If you are telling yourself that you are a 'bad girl' (or boy), the chances are that comes from childhood. But if your critical voice is blasting you for being a 'loser', it may belong to a teen peer or sibling. This identification process really helps to begin to take the power and credibility away from these inner tirades. Once you realise it is your granny, coach or school bitch who is giving you a hard time inside your head, then you can question it in the here and now with your rational adult brain.

Kirsty's critical choir

Kirsty the Lovely parent who we met in Chapter Three, was struggling with low confidence and self-esteem after three years of being a full-time mother. During the time of our therapy she decided to train as a massage therapist. It was hard to find the time and energy to fit this in with childcare and all her other responsibilities, but she managed to complete the course, get the client training hours and graduate.

One week Kirsty arrived for our appointment looking totally demoralised and dejected. She told me that the day before a terrible thing had happened to her and she had decided to give up her new career. 'What on earth happened?' I asked, imagining something dreadful. 'Well,' she said, 'I was queuing up in the bank to pay in my money from the first three weeks of business. It was only just over £200, but it felt like every penny was earned in blood.' Kirsty went on to explain that when she'd finally got to the front of the queue, she couldn't find the cash. She'd searched frantically in her pockets, handbag, even the secret compartment in her diary, but no luck. She told me that as she struggled to search for the money, the critical voices in her head reached a cacophony, 'like some crazed choir from hell'. 'What were they saying?' I asked. 'They said, "You are so stupid! Who do you think you are? Ha! I knew this would fail because you will fail at everything. And now everyone in this bank queue can see what a stupid loser you are. Ha ha ha ha!"'

Kirsty seemed to sink under the weight of remembering. 'The voices were so shrill and pitiless, mocking and remorseless,' she recalled with a shudder. She fell into a gloomy silence. 'It sounds like they are still on your shoulder,' I said. 'What can you think of to make them go away? Is there a benevolent voice you can access to counter them?' Kirsty thought for a bit, then a smile flickered across her face. 'Well my gran who has just passed away was always a big supporter of mine. She believed in me when others didn't.' She started to cry. 'What might she say to them?' I asked, gently.

There was a long pause, then Kirsty said in a loud northern accent: 'Bugger off and leave 'er alone, you big, nasty bullies – pick on someone yer own size!' Kirsty laughed: 'She was always quite salty, my gran. Said it like it was and didn't mind her Ps and Qs. But she always stood up for me.'

Kirsty left that day vowing to try and access her gran's voice whenever the vicious critics came into her head. She came back the following week with an even better plan: 'I'm now wearing her wedding ring on a gold chain around my neck. I touch it to help me access her love and support – and foul language!'

DISEMPOWER YOUR CRITICAL VOICES

As therapeutic ideas have developed, people have integrated the original concepts of Cognitive Behavioural Therapy (CBT) with other ideas to form what is called 'Third Wave CBT'. Many of these ideas use the centuries-old wisdom of Buddhist meditation, usually referred to as 'mindfulness'. One of these models is called Acceptance and Commitment Therapy (ACT) and a great book to read on this is *The Happiness Trap* by Russ Harris, an Australian GP with a very down-to-earth writing style. In his book, Russ describes many techniques you can use to separate from, observe, or even mock your critical thoughts and dialogue. These include putting them to the tune of a well-known song, like 'Happy Birthday', saying them in a comic voice or imagining them being broadcast on a radio, which you then switch off. One client who suffered from binge eating said she used this technique whenever she had had an eating spree. 'This is always followed by a whole heap of negative automatic thoughts that I'm disgusting, weak and fat, but then I began to challenge them by putting them into Homer Simpson's voice. I make it sound like Homer saying, "You're soooooo ugly". It really takes the edge off, makes me laugh a little and then I can let it go, or challenge it with reframing, depending on how repetitive the thoughts are.'

Other ACT techniques include recognising the thoughts – for example, 'I notice I'm having the thought that ...' to separate yourself from them, so you realise that they are not the *truth* and that you are a separate entity from them; or greeting them like old friends – 'Oh hello, you again!' – then thanking them for reminding you that you are a loser, fat, stupid (insert own negative, abusive thought here). Another idea is to 'Name that story' as in: 'Ah, the old "I'm-a-failure" story again'.

Former England International rugby player, Brian Moore, once said in an interview that he has suffered all his life from vicious critical voices that never allowed him to enjoy his sporting victories, telling him he's been lucky this time, but really he's a fraud and a failure. He explained how he has learnt to see them as belonging to Gollum (the traitor from *Lord of the Rings*); he said that he thanks him for his concern, then tells him 'but now bugger off and leave me alone'.

Another idea is to ask a powerful protector, either someone in your life now or from the past (like Kirsty's gran – see page 81), to speak to the critical thoughts on your behalf. Tell them to go away and to stop bullying you; maybe add an empowering compliment as well: 'You'll be brilliant, darling; I know you will. You can do it' – or whatever it is you need to see them off.

Mindful fighting

A few years ago I did an eight-week Mindfulness Meditation course at Bangor University (see Resources, page 218 to find a course near you). During the course, the two facilitators did a memorable role play. To symbolise how we often feel 'attacked' by our difficult or critical thoughts, one woman stood still while the other ran at her, fists flailing, as if to attack her. The woman under attack then demonstrated three different responses in a powerful visual representation of how we most frequently react to such attacking thoughts. The first was to just stand there and be pushed over (i.e. 'freeze'). But this did not make the assailant go away. Even as the 'victim' lay on the floor, her attacker continued to assault her. The second response was to try and run away, duck and dive and dodge to try and avoid the attacker (i.e. 'flight'). But of course she just chased her. And the third way was to fight back, which resulted in a big, noisy play fight. But one thing that was noticeable was that all three methods of dealing with the attacker involved a visible increase in energy. You could see it. And in the same way, the three ways in which we deal with critical attacking thoughts – basically a version of fight, flight or freeze – all increase the energy around the negative, attacking thoughts.

The women then demonstrated the mindful way of engaging with attacking thoughts: the victim turned towards her attacker, took her hands gently in her own and proceeded to dance with her, face to face, with her head up and an open posture. This represented compassionate curiosity – a phrase I love because it seems to me to encapsulate being active and open, yet kind and inquisitive. I have described this role play to many clients, and most love the idea of taking this attitude towards their difficult thoughts. They often practise compassionate curiosity using phrases similar to those suggested by Russ Harris, such as, 'Ah, you again. I wonder why you have appeared today?' – but in a gentle tone.

SHINE A LIGHT

Going back to the archaeology metaphor, once we have begun to recognise and bring compassionate curiosity to the vicious guardians that are our critical internal dialogue, then we can carefully bring the precious scrolls and ancient objects out into the light of day and shine a kindly torch of inquiry upon them. Ask yourself: where do they come from? Whose rules and beliefs are they? And, most importantly: do I still choose to believe them today as my most rational, aware adult self?

Beliefs are very powerful and are not necessarily just to do with our behaviour. Aaron Beck divided these up into three categories: beliefs we hold about ourselves, about others and about the world. He also differentiated between *conditional* beliefs, which come in the form of 'If (something) ... then (something else)' and *core* beliefs, which are usually deeply held and go to the core of who we believe we are (usually in the form of 'I *am* X or Y').

Monika and Ella uncover some rules and beliefs

With Monika, the '1000-watt light bulb' (see page 24), we worked with the ah-ha moment she had on her residential week, where she had managed to identify the anxiety in her body – the racing heart and dry mouth – and link it to how she had frequently felt around the family dining table (see page 63). 'I think the rule is something about keeping the peace, keeping everyone happy ... something like: I MUST TRY MY HARDEST TO SMOOTH OUT THE TENSIONS AND KEEP EVERYONE CALM.' 'Or else?' I asked. 'Or else I suppose I would suffer; I would be punished by my mum.' She also uncovered the conditional belief that 'If I don't give all my energy, then people won't like me'; beliefs about others – that 'women are jealous and dangerous', 'men and women hate each other'; about the world: 'you must fight for everything'; and core beliefs about herself – 'I am bad', 'I am unlovable'.

Ella, who felt socially crippled by 'the legacy of the mean girls', realised that she was increasingly editing out any mention of anything good in her own life in order to avoid provoking her supposed friends into sadness, anger or envy. 'What rules and beliefs are sitting at the bottom of that behaviour?' I asked her. Together, we uncovered the following list: 'I must not appear different from anyone', 'I must not draw attention to myself by voicing a different opinion', 'I must fit in and stay below the radar' and 'If I am not part of the group, I will never get a boyfriend'.

You may be reading this and thinking that Monika's and

Ella's thoughts are crazy and irrational, but that is the point: our ancient rules and beliefs usually *are* irrational because we believed them before we had developed the capacity for higher thinking processes, and when we had very little power over our own lives.

The Responsibility Pie

Here is an exercise to help you take another look at unhelpful beliefs about yourself that you may have carried around, unchallenged, since very early childhood. Beliefs such as 'It's all my responsibility' (say, to keep everyone happy) and, if the slightest thing goes wrong, then 'It's all my fault; I am to blame' or 'I am a bad girl/boy', etc.

You might remember pie charts from primary-school maths, but you can also think in terms of dividing a pie up into slices:

- Draw a circle on a piece of paper, then think of a key question about your life – something you feel responsible for and probably guilty that you didn't/don't do enough about.
- Now ask yourself: who is really responsible for this? Write the question down.
- Next, divide your pie into segments and write in each one the name of whoever owns that 'slice'. Do this quite quickly so that your subconscious can express its truth and your old 'shoulds' do not dictate the picture.

This is how Indira (see page 9) did the Responsibility Pie exercise. Her question was: who is responsible for looking after mum and dad? She divided her pie up giving 25 per cent each to her mum and dad. 'After all, they're not ill or infirm yet; they can mostly sort out their own stuff.' She divided the other half into four equal slices: one for each of her brothers, sister and herself. 'Just because I'm the only one who is not married or does not have kids, doesn't mean I'm the one who has to be on call twenty-four seven.'

This really helped Indira to realise that she did not have to feel obliged to always be the one to help, or feel guilty when she didn't. She wrote to her siblings explaining that she was about to be very busy finding a new job and embarking on internet dating, so they would have to take their share with their mum and dad. 'It was a bit stroppy,' she told me, 'but long overdue. In fact, I was amazed at how well most of them took it. It has given me a lot more space; both in my head and in my schedule.'

Often, when a client looks at a childhood issue in this way, they realise that they were not to blame *at all*. They have been carrying self-blame around – maybe that they deserved to be abused because they were bad or that their parents divorced because they were not good or lovable enough – but are amazed to see that they haven't given themselves a single slice of pie.

The old negative beliefs will not disappear overnight, but this can definitely begin to shift them. To realise as an adult that what we believed as a child was not the truth can be very liberating and profoundly change the way we think and act in the present. Indira had felt crushed by the weight of responsibility for her family, but with this lifted she felt she could breathe again and begin to take small, compassionate steps to regain her full alive self.

CHANGE YOUR SHOULDS TO COULDS

This has been one of the most consistently popular tools I have taught clients to use over the years. So many have said to me at the end of a series of sessions of tough emotional work – uncovering painful childhood memories, daring to confront parents and partners, bravely changing difficult aspects of their lives – that what helped them the most was 'That thing about should to could – that has been really life changing'. So I am passing it on here as a hot therapy favourite with many enthusiastic supporters.

The theory comes again from Aaron Beck's original CBT ideas. Beck writes that problematic emotional states such as anxiety and depression are, in part, caused by unhelpful thinking patterns – in particular the Rigid Personal Rules mentioned in Chapter One, which I think are vital to our understanding of why we think and behave as we do. These rules are 'black and white' or dichotomous because they give us no options – no shades of grey between them – for example, success or failure. For overburdened mother of three, Susie (see page 14), one of her Rigid Personal Rules was: I SHOULD ALWAYS BE A CALM AND LOVING MOTHER/I SHOULD NEVER SHOUT AT MY CHILDREN. When she did, inevitably, shout at one of her children, she would then feel terrible and a failure because she had broken her rule.

Worse than that though is the *meaning* of breaking your (impossible, perfectionist) Rigid Personal Rule. It meant to Susie that she was turning into her own mother which, in turn, meant (irrationally, of course) that her children would grow up hating her and never want to spend any time with her. Worse still, they would be severely psychologically and emotionally damaged; an image would even flash into Susie's mind (again, irrational) of her children grown up, destitute, homeless and begging in a cardboard box under Waterloo Bridge. These extreme thoughts and images keep us in a place of fear and I will talk more about them in Chapter Eight.

A more mundane example I often shared with my Holloway groups was a 'should' that often happened to me on those rushed working mornings, when I would run out of the house leaving a sink piled with unwashed breakfast stuff (and maybe some unwashed pans from the night before). I would say to myself, 'You *should* have done the washing up.' And as I hadn't, I would then berate myself with critical dialogue: 'You are such a lazy housekeeper; you are such a failure. You can't even organise yourself to wash the dishes. You are pathetic.'

Now what happens if you change the 'should' to a 'could' in that sentence? 'I *could* have done the washing up.' For me, that immediately introduces an element of choice. 'I *could* have done the washing up, but on this occasion I *chose* not to.' See how much easier that sounds? Did your shoulders drop down an inch when you read that gentle word 'could'? Because 'should' is a word that leads to self-beating almost by its very nature. It is a harsh word and, as such, it makes us very unhappy.

The shoulds are endless and can be about a whole range of subjects from what you 'should' be doing with your life ('I should be married', 'I should be successful', 'I should be famous by now' ...) to seemingly trivial matters, such as 'I should always wear lipstick' or 'I should always drink two litres of water each day'. There is nothing wrong with some of these ideas as *guidelines* by which to lead your life, but when they become rigid they have a tendency to become a cage in which you feel trapped.

The should of Elephant's Breath

A few years back, I paid for an interior designer to come round and advise me on what colours to paint my house. I think I must have been feeling particularly insecure at the time, or as my friend said, suffering from 'house shame'. Ten years before, when I had painted the walls in bright Mediterranean colours I had felt confident in my choices, but now I felt undermined and foolish as this terribly chic, contemporary woman, made slightly disparaging remarks about the 'nursery colours' and 'vibrant Mexican cantina look'. After a lot of sighing and holding up paint samples in various shades of grey, she delivered her verdict: 'I think you should paint the whole of the lower floor in Farrow & Ball Elephant's Breath.' Now to anyone from another planet, time or culture that is a puzzling, if not hilarious thought.

What colour would an elephant's breath be? Surely it would

be transparent, like most breath? But at the time, this was the height of chic and, believe me, F&B Elephant's Breath covered some of the trendiest walls in the land. So I dutifully bought the sample pot, painted a bit of lining paper and stuck it on the wall next to the telly. Where it tormented me for the *next three years*. Every time I flopped down after a long hard day for a bit of mindless TV comfort or escapism the thought came into my mind: you *should* paint this room in Elephant's Breath. And you can imagine all the other critical self-talk that accompanied that one 'should': this room is hideous; it looks like a Mexican cantina; you have no taste; you are an unsophisticated loser; you cannot invite anyone over the age of ten round until it has been repainted in F&B EB, etc. It is no exaggeration to say that giving my power away to the opinion of that chic lady and believing her judgment over my own sucked the joy out of that room – almost the entire house – for three whole years. (In case you are curious, I have now regained the belief in my own judgment and painted the rooms in a lovely, unfashionable pale chalky blue, which helps me feel peaceful and sunny.)

For Lovelies, the shoulds can create the feeling of being trapped in a cage of our own making, and one that we don't know how to begin to dismantle. So much of this is about insecurity and comparison. When we feel certain of who we are and what our values, tastes and standards are, then we don't care what others think of the colour of our lounge walls, the state of the sink or our children's GCSE results. But of course, in this modern world of advanced consumerism, where marketing can make us feel inadequate and inferior in so many ways (so that we will buy the products and services to make us feel 'right'), then it is a rare person who manages to feel secure and 'right' in themselves in all aspects of their life.

Catch your shoulds

Try this experiment. I would like you, just for one day, to try and catch yourself when you use the word 'should' (to yourself and to others). See if you can catch it in time to change it to 'could', and observe what happens to your thoughts, feelings and behaviour when you do so. If you like, you could do this for more than a day and note down the results in your notebook. But that's not a 'should' ...

Here is a range of shoulds that I have collected from observing myself and my clients over the years:

- I should paint the lounge in Elephant's Breath.

- I should lose half a stone.

- I should be fitter.

- I should eat my five portions of fruit and veg every day.

- I should have sex with my partner more often.

- I should have stopped grieving by now.

- I should be married at this age.

- I should brush my teeth twice a day.

- I should ring my mother more often.

YOUR PERSONAL BILL OF RIGHTS

Before you can change your behaviour and act in different ways, it is vital that you begin to believe that you have *the right* to do this. The United States of America has its Bill of Rights, which guarantees a number of personal freedoms and seems to be an integral part of citizenship, taught in schools and known to most. The first time I was really aware that we all have a *personal* Bill of Rights was when I read Anne Dickson's book, *A Woman in Your Own Right*, in which she lists eleven basic human rights. They can sound very obvious and simplistic, but you may have never really considered them before, and you may – subconsciously – hold your own set of beliefs drawn from childhood or society that counters these rights, thus making it hard to believe they actually apply to you.

The Personal Bill of Rights includes:

- I have the right to express my feelings, opinions and values.

- I have the right to be me.

- I have the right to say no.

- I have the right to make mistakes.

- I have the right to change my mind.

- I have the right to say I don't understand.

- I have the right not to feel responsible for the problems of other adults.

- I have the right to put myself first.

- I have the right not to be dependent on the approval of others.

The Personal Bill of Rights begins to prepare you for the next chapter, which is about not just saying to yourself that you have the right to do something different, but helping to reinforce these new, helpful beliefs in practical ways by behaving differently towards yourself.

SUMMARY

This chapter has suggested some practical ideas to help you identify and challenge the personal rules and beliefs that underpin the Curse of Lovely.

- Question your critical thoughts and 'ancient' personal rules.

- Disempower your critical voices.

- Try the 'Responsibility Pie' exercise (page 87) to help you view some of your beliefs in a new light.

- Change your 'shoulds' to 'coulds'.

- Become familiar with your Personal Bill of Rights.

CHAPTER SIX

Because I'm Worth It –
Being Lovely to Ourselves

Lovelies generally have a low sense of self-worth and self-esteem and we are often very dependent on the approval of others to make us feel good about ourselves. Remember Carl Rogers' idea of the internal versus the external locus of evaluation in Chapter Two (see page 31)? Well, as Lovelies we generally need to work on building up our internal locus – the one that comes from the opinion of ourselves, not others.

Most of us know someone who either amazes or irritates us because they seem to have a very strong sense of personal entitlement? Well, we need a bit of what they have, and I'm going to share some of the ways to try and achieve that. People vary widely as to what works for them, so try to be open-minded and see what you think you might be able to try.

THE ARC OF REDEMPTION

A friend of mine who is a screenwriter first alerted me to this idea. 'Hollywood demands that every story has what is called an Arc of Redemption,' he explained. 'That means, for example, the classic boy meets girl, boy loses girl, boy gets girl in the end. The redemptive part is that one or both of them undergoes a dramatic character change, usually a blinding insight or ah-ha moment that enables them to proceed to the happy ending. We, the audience, often know it before they do, which adds to the dramatic will-they-won't-they tension.' He told me that it is not just full-length movies that must follow the Arc of Redemption, but that every episode of a series like the mega-successful *Friends*, for example, has its own mini arc – often within a bigger arc that spans many episodes, such as will/won't Rachel and Ross get together? If you watch films or TV with this in mind, you will start to notice how often it happens (although there are, of course, noticeable exceptions – usually movies labelled as 'dark' or 'art-house', which tend to be more true to real life).

The problem with the Arc of Redemption is that it creates a false hope in us all. We have generally swallowed so much of this stuff by the time we are young adults that we invest a great deal in the expectation that the people we love, but who often disappoint us and don't love us in the ways we would want, will have their moment of epiphany or blinding flash of insight, and suddenly love and appreciate us in the ways we'd hoped for. This, of course, rarely happens because people change slowly, if at all. As Brad Pitt said in a recent interview:

'When I started in film I was taught that you had to have a character arc and there had to be an epiphany. As years go by, I have found that to be utter bullshit. We don't really change; we evolve by degrees.'

Nevertheless, our investment in this idea is huge, and can often stop us changing ourselves (the only change that *is* under our control), as we wait for others to become who we want them to be. I have found that this does not just apply to romantic partners, but seems to hold a particularly powerful grip when it comes to parents, and, to a lesser extent, siblings and, of course, friends.

When I spot this with clients and ask them to describe their hope for their parent or sibling it almost always includes the idea that they will a) apologise for the wrong they have done them and b) affirm their love and pride. The dream speech goes something like, 'Darling, I know I have been a bad mother/father/brother/partner over the years and have made terrible mistakes, but I love you more than anything, and am so proud of you. Please forgive me and let us start again.'

Be your own redemption

To paraphrase the Serenity Prayer used by recovery support groups: if we put our energies into trying to change what we can change (and accept what we can't, and have the wisdom to know the difference between the two), then we can begin to bring about our *own*, gradual and gentle, redemption.

A large part of bringing about our own redemption is to

give ourselves the love and care we are secretly hoping others will give us. A BBC television series, *The Convent*, sent a group of women to a nunnery to see if this could help them sort out their troubled lives in some way. A memorable scene sticks in my mind of one woman who was very unhappy and constantly crying. She had already revealed that she had had a wretched childhood with an alcoholic father and a harsh and critical mother. She now had four of her own children and at times felt suicidal, and wanted to find a way to peace. She was filmed having a one-to-one session with a softly-spoken nun who looked about ninety-two and radiated wisdom and compassion. 'I'm sure you are a good mother to your little ones,' said the kindly nun (or words to this effect). 'Now you need to mother yourself like you would one of your beloved children. Give her comfort when she is frightened, words of encouragement and good food and rest. You have the skills; you must use them on yourself too.' The woman had never even had this thought, but could see how it might help. It was very moving, as she wept buckets and confessed that she had carried on being a harsh, critical mother to herself (like her own mum), but liked the idea of trying to be the kind, loving mother she was to her children, to herself.

I don't think you have to have children to access these skills and qualities. Think of the small children you are fond of (maybe relatives or godchildren) and how you are with them – what you say to them when they are upset or frightened. The love and care you show to pets is also a good model. Basically, try and be to yourself the loving, approving parent you crave others to be.

EXTREME SELF-CARE

A book I have grown to love is Cheryl Richardson's *The Art of Extreme Self-Care*. The title is thought provoking in itself as it points up nicely that there is a real sense of risk, danger and fear in the idea of caring for ourselves properly. The idea of maybe recognising and putting our own needs first, even some of the time, feels so risky it is analogous to a so-called 'extreme' sport, like paragliding or bungee jumping.

Affirmations

One of Cheryl's more challenging suggestions is that you build up your self-love by, literally, telling yourself you love yourself every day. Look in the mirror every morning and say: 'I love you (insert your own name)'. And don't snigger! How hard is that even to *read*, let alone do? I'm afraid that while I could certainly see the value in this, I fell at the first hurdle, so high were my own defence mechanisms. But one of my very intellectual, highly professional clients actually made herself do it. She said it was one of the hardest things she has ever done (and she has degrees from the world's top universities), but that it was also incredibly transforming. She had been going through a rough time on almost all fronts – divorce; severely dysfunctional, unsupportive family; stress at work; illness and death of a beloved relative – and was barely hanging in there. She told me: 'Someone said to me the other day, "You look happy", and I realised that I *had* woken up that morning feeling happy for the first time in about eighteen months.' Of course, she was in therapy and making other shifts in her life and relationships, but she felt that saying 'I love you Rebecca' to herself every morning and every night in the mirror was key to her shift in wellbeing.

The 'I love you' affirmation above is possibly the most challenging one I have encountered, but you can create any affirmation you want to address how you are trying to change. When I taught the psychological courses at Holloway Prison, affirmations were surprisingly popular and effective. One of the favourites with my groups was, 'I am breaking old patterns and moving forward.' The women loved that one because it was positive and uplifting, yet also truthful for most of them.

The only guideline when formulating an affirmation is that it helps if you start it with 'I am', followed by something positive and in the present tense. So you might say, 'I am learning to be kind and loving to myself' or 'I am learning to say no to things that drain my energy' or simply 'I am a good person'. It also helps to say the affirmation out loud or in your head; for maximum effect, say it while looking directly at yourself in the mirror, and as often as you can.

Three-good-things-a-day Diary

As I said earlier, many of us reach adulthood finding it difficult to think good things about ourselves. Being harsh and self-critical has become a habit of thinking encoded into the neural pathways of our brain. It is the default setting on our personal self-talk computer. Keeping a Three-good-things-a-day Diary (or simply entering them into your phone) will help you develop kinder, more helpful habits of thinking. It is important that you can begin to notice the good qualities that you have and give yourself praise and credit for them. It's part of being your own redemption – you have to do it for yourself first.

This theory comes from the Positive Psychology movement which was created by Martin Seligman and others in the 1990s to focus on noticing and building our strengths and resilience, rather than focusing on weaknesses and deficiencies. The movement built up a substantial body of research-based evidence to show that changing focus on to positives can bring about significant improvements in mental health. By making yourself actually write down these positive thoughts in your Three-good-things-a-day Diary, it is possible to create new neural pathways in the brain. The idea is that after a couple of weeks of diligently recording at least one good thing you have done every day (it doesn't matter if you can't find three to start with), you can just think the new, helpful thoughts about yourself without having to write them down.

Although clients generally really struggle to do this, those who have persevered have reported that is has a very powerful effect on their sense of self-worth and self-esteem. It is not as hard as it sounds when you realise you can include all kinds of actions and tasks that you might otherwise dismiss ('Oh, anyone would have done that') or take for granted ('But I have to cook the dinner anyway'). It is the *ordinary*, not the extraordinary, that you are looking to notice.

For each 'event' you record, write down the personal qualities that this shows you have. For example, 'I bought some daffodils for my table. I am creative, thoughtful, loving.' It helps to think how you might generously describe a good friend who had performed the same action. Keep this record private to help overcome the potential barrage of critical voices that will be dismissing every positive thought you have about yourself as trivial, ridiculous, big-headed, boastful, etc. It might also help to use the ideas I introduced in the previous chapter to challenge your critical voices when they do arise (see pages 78–83).

Here are some Three-good-things-a-day Diary entries generously shared by several clients to give you some inspiration:

- Went to work, even though I felt ill. I am reliable and conscientious.

- Tried to support father on the phone with difficulties he was having. I am supportive, caring, truthful and determined to help.

- I tried really hard in a sport when it was easy to not try and just be there for the social part. I am determined and inspired.

- Wrote up study schedule. I am organised and willing to succeed.

- Sang in a performance. I am confident, appreciative and committed.

- Met with ex-boyfriend. Was compassionate and forgiving. Listened without judgment when he talked about relationship with my former best friend.

- Did an interview in sign language today for a job that scares me. Feel proud that I stayed calm and did it anyway. I am brave.

- A neighbour came round who I had never met, needing help examining her throat. She was embarrassed, so I made her feel at ease and put her mind at rest regarding her throat. Strangers make me nervous, but I was still very friendly to her and helpful.

- Asked line manager for meeting. Told her my workload was too much and asked what we could do about this. She was amazingly helpful and said she had had no idea it had been a problem. I was brave and honest. Dared to ask for help.

- Cooked a new recipe from the *Jamie* book. The kids didn't like it, but I stayed calm. I am adventurous and choosing life and health.

- Watched TV programme with my daughter; we cuddled up and laughed together. I am a good father and made the time for some bonding.

- Didn't go to F's gig at last minute as too tired. Good call! Am looking after myself well and can always go to the next one. Great to wake up without hangover.

- Didn't buy designer top in sale as was embarrassed in front of friend. Rang up today and bought over the phone. I acted quickly to correct a mistake. I am dynamic, resourceful and overcame feeling that I'm not worth it.

- Helped sort out squabble between T and J. I am a creative problem-solver and a good mum.

- Helped friend look at flatting options differently. I am a good listener, interested in my friends and keen to help them, perceptive, thoughtful, objective, able to offer suggestions and come up with new ideas.

- Bought a Three-good-things-a-day Diary for my cousin and wrote in the first three entries of qualities I notice in her. I am caring, supportive, generous, positive, wanting to help her see her own good features.

- Cheered up four-year-old god-daughter by giving her horse rides on my knee. I am fun, able to relate to children, uninhibited, thoughtful, kind and a bit silly!

The client who shared those last three examples said that she wrote them down every night before she went to sleep, and that focusing on the positive things seemed to lead to a much better night's rest: 'Before, I would have unsolved problems and critical thoughts swirling around my head which made it very difficult to drift off; but doing the Three-good-things Diary puts me in a much less anxious place to sleep.' After keeping the diary for two and a half weeks, this young woman said that it had made a huge difference to how she felt about herself. 'For me, it has changed what my brain is looking for throughout the day. Instead of beating myself up and confirming "You're so crap", the lens I am looking through has kind of changed, so I am looking for "What am I happy with?"'

Keeping this record, even if you only do it occasionally, helps build up a resource that you can turn to in times of difficulty and self-doubt. You can read back over the entries and remember when and why you felt good about yourself. Most Lovelies seem to have a powerful taboo against self-praise that makes them very resistant to this exercise. But persevere – the pay-off is powerful.

The tea-for-one breakthrough

One of my first ever clients was an incredibly intelligent, high-flying career woman and mother of three small children who never *ever* did anything just for herself. After about six months of therapy (she rationalised that this was to improve things for her children) during which she worked extremely diligently to uncover the patterns of thoughts, feelings and behaviour that had brought her to a grinding but functioning depression, she turned up looking elated. 'I have had a breakthrough!' she announced, beaming. I was literally on the edge of my seat with anticipation. What could she have done to cause such obvious joy? 'I have bought a tea-for-one set,' she declared. I imagine that I must have looked stunned, having never even heard of a tea-for-one set (although I subsequently went out and bought one for myself). 'What is it?' I asked. And my client went on to describe a small teapot which sits on top of a matching cup and saucer. 'It holds enough for two cups,' she said, then added, with a mischievous smile, 'but it's just for me.'

This was definitely a turning point for this self-sacrificing woman. It broke the Rigid Personal Rule I MUST NEVER PUT MY OWN NEEDS BEFORE MY FAMILY'S (... or something terrible would happen, as it had done in her childhood). With this seemingly trivial yet incredibly brave experiment, she managed to begin to break the hold of this powerful belief. We could say that her adult rational brain showed her superstitious inner-child brain that a small treat for herself would not cause tragedy for her family. It opened the way to further experimenting, including taking time off to go on 'artist's dates' to nurture her creativity (as suggested by the excellent book *The Artist's Way* by Julia Cameron) and investigating downsizing in order to work part-time, see her children more and develop her creative writing.

HOW CAN *YOU* TREAT YOURSELF?

The beauty brand L'Oreal rather monopolised an important idea when they created the slogan 'Because You're Worth It'. It goes back to that idea of entitlement again. Go on, they urge, buy this lovely hair product; you have great and precious value as a wonderful human being and should treat yourself to the very best. Only many of us completely struggle to feel, on a very deep level, that we can spend time, energy, money and *love* on ourselves. We actually feel the very opposite of what L'Oreal tell us: that we are not really worth anything very good or special. And so often, as I have said before, Lovelies give away their time, energy, money and love to others and don't spend any on themselves. But now, for the sake of your sanity, health, happiness and wellbeing, I am encouraging you to do just that.

So what is your equivalent of the tea-for-one set? It's not easy to suggest ideas, as one person's pampering is another's poison, but some of my clients' examples include: swimming, taking luxurious baths, rollerblading, dancing (tap, zumba, ballroom, salsa), running (marathons or just around the park), writing, painting, visiting art galleries, going to music festivals, horse riding, dog walking, massage, joining choirs, arranging activities with friends (rather than evenings spent drinking wine and talking about problems), being in nature, being by water ... the list is endless and it is highly personal. I encourage people to think back to things they remember enjoying as a child or young adult, and to see if they can find a way of doing them now. It might take a slightly different form – say, a dance-exercise class instead of clubbing – but it can bring about the same feelings of joy and freedom, which are both empowering and nurturing.

The client who felt her sense of self-worth was transformed by the Three-good-things-a-day Diary also put a lot of effort into finding activities which would increase her sense of fun and sensual pleasure. She had been ignoring or punishing her body for years with a combination of high academic achievement, long, hard office hours, a joyless gym schedule and a starve-binge eating pattern. Four months into our therapy, she had made the following changes: she took up badminton lessons, which were fun and social; she signed up for a mindfulness course and yoga sessions; she went on a week-long Fit Farm residential which showed her ideas for enjoyable and healthy eating and exercise; and, finally, she went to an introductory tantric sex workshop. She also bought gorgeously scented bath and body products and delicious healthy food to treat herself and her senses. When I saw her after a bank-holiday break she was glowing with life force, energy and excitement. She thanked me for letting her find these new interests at her own pace: 'If you had said in the first few sessions you *must* do these things, I would have totally resisted and never done them. But instead, you just told me to keep an eye out for what makes my energy rise, and that's what I've followed.'

So what makes your energy rise? This may sound a little obscure to start with, but it goes back to the ideas in Chapter Four about tuning in to what your body is telling you. When someone makes a suggestion or request of you, chances are that something in your body responds positively or negatively – I call this energy rising or falling. (For many people this feeling is in their stomach, hence the expression 'gut reaction'.) It happens almost instantaneously, and often we don't notice it or we override it.

In looking for activities that will build up your positive sense of self, gently monitor where your attention is drawn to and what makes your interest – or energy – rise. Then, at your own pace, start putting these clues from your body (or possibly your subconscious) into practice. What activity do you feel drawn to and want to have a go at? Try and schedule things in advance in your diary and don't change them because other people ask you to do things. Prioritise yourself for a change and see how that begins to slowly shift deeply held beliefs about your value and worth.

Rate your day

One of the ideas I loved from the mindfulness meditation course I attended a few years ago (see Resources, page 218) was the 'Rate Your Day' exercise. I have since taught it to many clients who have found that it is simple, but very effective. Here's what you do:

- Make a list of every task and activity in your day, then rate them as either draining, mastery (when you feel competent) or pleasurable, by putting the letter D, M or P next to each one.

- Next, think of how can you change some of the items that you feel are draining into being either pleasurable or mastery.

People on the course came up with all sorts of suggestions, but what was interesting was to see how one person's draining was another's pleasurable. For example, emails for many were draining, but some said mastery because they feel good when they have done them. One woman even said that emails to her are pleasurable because she never knows who may have contacted her and what surprises and adventures might be waiting in her inbox. Another I remember was commuting – many said this was draining, but someone suggested that if you listen to some favourite music, a podcast or read a book of your choice it can become pleasurable. Others included taking time to really smell and taste your favourite drink in the morning, using a beautifully scented shower gel and savouring the smell, rubbing in body lotion and enjoying the sensation, looking at nature around you when you get the chance, hearing birdsong when you leave home in the morning . . .

A lot of it is about using our five senses. Often, we seem to ignore smell, touch, taste and hearing as we focus predominantly on our power of sight. And often, we grit our teeth, switch off our sensory awareness and just get through things that have to be done, thus depriving ourselves of a possible richness of experience, or even unexpected pleasure.

Speak to your inner child

This goes back to the idea behind what the nun advised the desperate woman on the television series I mentioned earlier (see page 99), but it goes a step further and you actually engage with your younger self as if she/he were in the room with you.

The first time I tried doing this was after taking the advice of my clinical supervisor, Dr Lynne Jordan. I had been talking about a particularly angry client who scared me to the point where I dreaded her sessions, even though I could also feel that she was a human being in pain and suffering who deserved my help. 'It is your inner child that is frightened,' said Lynne. 'What could you say to her to make her feel safe before this client arrives?' What a completely bonkers question I thought (secretly, of course, editing my true thoughts in classic Lovely style). 'I haven't a clue,' I replied. 'How about something like: that scary client is about to arrive, why don't you go and play in the other room and I'll take care of the situation,' Lynne suggested in her straight-forward manner.

I went away completely unconvinced. But I remembered the idea just before the client arrived the following week and thought, nothing to lose – might as well give it a go. So I duly told my inner child (I pictured myself aged about three) that I would deal with the scary grown-up stuff, that she could go and play or take a nap in the other room and that I would keep her safe. And guess what? It worked a treat. I think it separated the pre-logical reasoning part of my brain – the part I have named Toddler Terror (a historically huge fear of anger, conflict, con-frontation and disapproval) – from my adult rational reasoning capacity; so I was able to sit in my consulting room and use all my grown-up training, skills and expertise, while little (fright-ened) Jacqui was safe (metaphorically) in the 'other room'.

I have since shared this idea with many clients, and because for many sufferers of the Curse of Lovely, there is often a ver-sion of Toddler Terror at work, talking in a soothing way to help their inner child feel safe is a very practical and helpful strategy. But for some Lovelies, the traumatic time in their life was their teenage years, so for them it could be more helpful to talk to their inner teen.

Sarah talks to her teen self

Sarah, who we met in Chapter Two, felt stuck in her life, partly because of the limiting beliefs she had acquired in her difficult teen years when she had been the 'fat-but-nice friend', always assuming that boys simply talked to her to get to her gorgeous best friend. She agreed to speak to her fifteen-year-old self in the safety of a therapy session to see if that might help shift things a bit.

Like most clients I suggest this to Sarah was embarrassed and sceptical at first. I asked her to imagine her younger self on the spare chair in the room, to shut her eyes, visualise and speak to young Sarah. 'Can you tell her three nice things about herself?' I asked. 'Considerate, giving and quite positive,' she said quickly. I told her I thought she could say more: 'Sarah aged fifteen is sitting there and wants to know what boys could possibly see in her. You are her fairy godmother – what do you say?' She laughed, then said, 'Sarah, it's going to turn out all right. It's not ultimately about looks. You're passionate, fun and interesting. People like you and that will take you a very long way.'

Sarah later said that this was one of the toughest things she had ever done. 'It was so painful. But I've tried to use it in a positive way and I've been thinking of that girl as a separate person, one who I'm trying to help.'

Sarah increased her exercise regime and cut down on alcohol. Her new aim was to have a few social drinks, but not to be the last one at the party. 'I used to tell people that I have no personality without Pinot Grigio, but I know that's not true. My fun side is really there all the time. People like me in the office and I know I add to the room.' She signed up for a fun run and joined a running club where she slowly (very slowly) began to realise that some men seemed interested in her despite her being stone-cold sober, dressed in jogging bottoms and with sweat dripping into her eyes.

Talking to your inner child or teen is not a one-off therapy trick. Whenever you feel a stab of anxiety, chances are it is being triggered by your Toddler (or Teen) Terror. At these points, remembering to have a soothing word with this younger self can, almost miraculously, make you feel calmer and allow you to access your creative, problem-solving adult brain.

A friend of mine who was going through a particularly traumatic break-up and feeling abandoned and alone said she would drive around in the car and take the imaginary hand of her six-year-old self (the age she was when her own parents divorced) as if she was sitting in the passenger seat beside her. 'There, there,' she would say, lovingly. 'It's all going to be all right. I will look after you.'

SUMMARY

In this chapter I have described a number of techniques that can help you begin to value yourself more. Here is a reminder:

- Think about becoming your own 'redemption' and giving yourself the love and kindness you keep hoping others will give to you.

- Try formulating positive affirmations about yourself and saying them regularly (though privately).

- Keep a Three-good-things-a-day Diary to notice and praise what you do well.

- Think of ways you can treat yourself – and enjoy them *without guilt*.

- Rate the activities of your day with a 'D' for 'draining', 'M' for 'mastery' or 'P' for pleasurable', then think of simple ways in which you could change some of the Ds to Ms or Ps.

- Try speaking soothingly and encouragingly to your inner child or teen when you feel anxious or alone.

CHAPTER SEVEN

Polish Your Tools

The other day, one of my clients was talking about a difficult conversation she needed to have. She wanted to object about some training provided by her company that she felt had been badly run and had undermined her confidence. 'I want to complain to HR, but I don't know how to do it appropriately. I'm so scared of getting it wrong and being punished somehow. It's like I need your help to select the right tool from my tool kit.'

I thought that was such a good metaphor that we played around with it for a while. What kind of tool did she think she needed for this job? 'Well,' she said thoughtfully, 'it feels quite delicate, so I probably need something like a small screwdriver. But while I'm trying to choose the right one, I'm scared I'll pick up the chainsaw and there will be a huge massacre. Blood everywhere, like in the movie!'

So here is an inventory of some of the tools you may find helpful as you begin to plan and prepare to act and communicate in ways that are new and different. Some of them you probably know already, some may be new to you. The choice is highly personal, so select those that you think will be of most use to you in the situation you are about to encounter. Then, remember to keep them polished and ready in your tool kit.

ACCESS YOUR BRAVEST SELF

One of my favourite therapy exercises is called the Dependable Strengths Inventory. I came across it when I studied Personal Construct Psychology (developed by George Kelly in the 1960s) and modified it to use with my Holloway prison groups.

Kelly's central idea is that we all have 'strengths' (some might call them 'resiliences') and that these are 'dependable' throughout our lives – they are always there for us to access, even if they have lain dormant for a while in a period of our lives when we have not felt very strong. The exercise helps you to identify these qualities and make an 'inventory' – or list – of them, which you can then access in times of crisis when you need a confidence boost. In that way, it is very similar to the Three-good-things-a-day Diary introduced in the last chapter, but it draws on personal evidence from the past, rather than the present.

Think of times in your past when you have done something you are proud of, however insignificant these might seem to others. It could be helping a friend, sticking at something difficult or having your work put up on the wall at school. Try and list at least three, then next to them write the qualities (or dependable strengths) that they show you possess. There is always something to identify. For example, by buying and reading this book you are trying to change something you are not happy with in your life. That shows the qualities of determination, proactivity and courage. Don't let your critical voices dismiss your ideas.

BE YOUR OWN CHEERLEADER

This is like putting your Dependable Strengths into a simple, encouraging affirmation, suitable for the occasion. What phrase or slogan can you say to yourself before you make that difficult call, face that difficult person or find yourself in a difficult situation requiring greater assertiveness?

One of my workshop participants came up with the following words to say to herself when faced with a stroppy (young) service provider: 'Come on, you can do this! You are old enough to be their mother. It will be fine.' Others evoked their supportive person (like Kirsty's gran in the 'Disempowering your critical voices' exercise on page 81), with phrases like: 'You are great! Go for it!' It can also be really helpful to remind yourself of the Personal Bill of Rights we looked at in Chapter Five. Saying to yourself something like, 'I have the right to put myself first' or 'I have the right to say no' can be very empowering at a critical moment.

BODY LANGUAGE

Research has consistently shown that we read more information from each other via non-verbal communication – or body language – than anything else. Pioneer body language researcher Albert Mehrabian put the balance at approximately 55 per cent body language, 38 per cent vocal (especially tone of voice) and only 7 per cent the actual words spoken.

So when you are thinking of saying something different from your normal type of communication, which therefore feels very difficult, it can be helpful to focus on the messages your face, body and voice are giving out before you even start to think of the actual words you might need to use.

Posture

If you stand up tall and straight and look people in the eye, then you will feel more confident and radiate confidence to others. If you have a difficult phone call to make, try standing up while you do it. This will make you feel stronger and this, in turn, will come across in your voice. Similarly, if your boss comes over to your desk to speak to you, it can be helpful to stand up, so you are speaking eye to eye and do not feel at a disadvantage, literally being spoken down to.

In my Holloway assertiveness groups we used to do an exercise where the women would walk around the room with slumping posture, eyes to the ground, etc., then I would ask them to walk tall and make eye contact. They reported that the difference they felt in their bodies was noticeable: they felt better, stronger and more confident as they walked around pretending to be so. 'Fake it till you make it, eh Miss?' as one prisoner said (with no irony, considering she was on a fraud charge).

Parenting classes I attended when my children were small taught a similar posture idea to communicate calm authority to children: 'Imagine you are a magnificent tree, or a rock,' the tutor said. 'Stand strong and firm, rooted into the earth.' I found the tree image particularly helpful as it means you are rooted in the ground, yet not totally inflexible.

If you have ever done drama, movement, dance, yoga or Pilates classes, you have probably been taught how to pull up your stomach (or core) muscles, put your shoulders back and imagine a golden thread pulling up from the top of your head to achieve upright posture. You can use this method or, again, whatever works best for you.

Micro-signals

These are what people like police interviewers and poker players look for to check if suspects or opponents are telling the truth. They can tell from tiny changes in the face, especially the eyes, when there is an inconsistency – or mismatch – between what people are saying and what they are really thinking.

When you have to say something difficult, try and be aware of the messages your face and body might be giving off that do not tally with the words you are saying. Try to hold steady eye contact, not to fidget and not to play with your mouth or ears.

Taking some slow, deep breaths will help remove the tension from your face, eyes and jaw.

Ration that wonderful smile

Of course, one of the biggest micro-signals that can suggest we do not mean what we are saying is our smile.

Now, I am not knocking your smile. You probably consider it one of your best assets, and may have often been told so. I have smiled constantly most of my life, and it has undoubtedly opened many doors for me. (It has also cost me a fortune in anti-wrinkle creams, as the habit is etched firmly into my skin in deep crows' feet and now lines around my mouth too that make me look like a wooden puppet.)

Most Lovelies tend to over-smile. It is usually a deeply ingrained habit, and we often think this is our best bet for getting our needs met: I smile; you like me; you will want to be nice to me and help me out. We also know, on some level that it makes people feel safe: it is argued that the evolutionary origins of the smile are in the monkeys that peel back their upper lips and bare their teeth to signal that they are not a threat to aggressors seeking a fight – a non-verbal sign of submission.

So while there is nothing wrong with your wonderful smile – many people would die for it – you need to have options and you need to practise them. Can you smile when you *choose* to? More importantly, can you choose *not* to smile?

When my friend Hilary was at secondary-school teacher-training college the trainee teachers were warned that they would give the wrong message if they smiled too much in the classroom – that the students would think they were a 'soft touch' and a pushover and, before they knew it, they would have lost control and authority, which is very difficult to regain. So they were told to be very aware of their facial expressions when in front of the class. The advice Hilary found most memorable and helpful, especially in her first job in a challenging comprehensive was, 'Never smile before Christmas.' What this meant was that when you start in September, pretend you are a sterner, less accommodating version of yourself for the whole of the first term to establish authority and, hopefully, win respect. Then, maybe, you can start to show your real self a little more in the second term – i.e. after Christmas – including the occasional smile. Hilary, a naturally enthusiastic, smiley person, found this invaluable. 'It's quite a common game for a class to try and make the new teacher "lose it", so using authoritative body language definitely helped me keep control,' she told me.

Parenting lessons give similar advice. 'Pretend to be cross before you are really angry,' Tamar, the teacher at the parenting classes I attended told us. 'When we are angry we are already out of control, and this is frightening both to ourselves and to the child, who senses the danger in the unpredictable behaviour that comes with the adult having lost control.' In parenting-class role plays I would try and say something serious ('Bedtime. Now'), then ruin it with a pleading smile. 'You are sending out a mixed message by smiling at the end,' said Tamar. 'You don't have to be mean or nasty. Just say it in a calm, even tone. And don't smile at the end. You are telling, not pleading.' This was so difficult for me (and several others in the group) to start with. But when practised, and especially in conjunction with posture ('I am a rock') and the Stuck-record Technique (see page 129), it is surprisingly possible and amazingly effective. Now, fifteen years on, when kids come round for a sleepover, I deliver a short, low-toned speech about house rules, with a serious face. And they seem fine about it. They know where they stand and it is probably preferable to encountering a screaming, sleep-deprived mummy at 3am when they decide to raid the fridge.

VERBAL COMMUNICATION

Cut out the waffle

Try and be direct: cut out the waffle and the long-winded back story. We often confuse speaking clearly and directly with being blunt and rude. We live in a culture where indirect communication is often the norm – especially for women – hinting, guilt-tripping and charming people into responding to our unexpressed needs. And then maybe sulking, complaining or being sarcastic when they don't. Often, the last thing we do is actually *say* what we want.

I used to do this a lot when I had something difficult to say or ask and Jocelyn Chaplin, my inspiring therapist, was the first person who ever directly (calmly and clearly) pointed it out to me. Once, when I was trying to change a therapy appointment, I spent about ten minutes telling her a long, involved story about how it was going to be half-term and I had to take one of my sons to the airport as he was going to visit his friend in Spain and blah, blah, waffle, waffle . . . all the while looking down, looking away, not holding eye contact, looking up occasionally to smile in a winning (pleading?) manner. At the end of my story she looked me in the eye and said, 'Jacqui, I don't know what you're asking me.' I probably looked a bit baffled and hurt, so she added, very gently, 'What is it you want to ask me? Can you say it clearly?' I paused and thought. (This is one of the great benefits of therapy; it is a safe space where you can practise doing things in a different way, especially regarding how you act and communicate in relationship to another human being.) I realised that it felt very risky to ask her for something directly; I suppose the risk lay in feeling that she might be angry with me for asking for what I wanted. But I took a few deep breaths, rehearsed in my head what is was that I actually wanted to ask – in one clear sentence – and finally, said, 'Jocelyn, can we rearrange next week's appointment to later in the day, say 1pm?' As far as I can remember, she actually said no, that would not be possible, but that I could cancel completely.

We then talked about the effect on the other person when we obfuscate and pad out requests or refusals with irrelevant facts and waffle. (Think of how it is when you yourself are on the receiving end of a long, drawn-out request or refusal.) It is confusing and puzzling. Sometimes, by the end, we are uncertain as to what it is we are being asked or told, and sometimes we have lost the plot, feel bored and our mind has wandered to what's on television tonight.

Finding the right words

Much of our problem with not being able to refuse a request, or ask for what we actually want, stems from not knowing the words to say, and having little or no practice in actually saying them.

I recently met an old friend of mine who is a very dynamic and successful businesswoman; she has started up and run many ventures in the eighteen years I've known her and employed many people. She was on her way to meet a new contact who was offering her some consultancy work. 'How much are you charging him?' I asked, conversationally. She looked embarrassed and a bit frozen, like when you ask your six-year-old if they have changed their pants. There was an awkward silence while she fidgeted and looked at the floor. 'You haven't discussed it have you?' I asked, amazed. 'I can't do it,' she said. 'I can do it readily for others, but not for myself.'

We then did a role play where I asked her to calmly and clearly look me in the eye and say something like, 'My current consultancy fee is £500 a day.' But there was no way she could say this comfortably, so we compromised with, 'What would you expect to pay for this work?' Actually, she couldn't even bring herself to use the word 'pay', so we settled on 'What would be the normal day rate for this work?' She texted later to say the meeting had gone really well and it had been relatively easy to say the words having rehearsed them with me. 'It's just getting them past your lips for the first time – they seemed stuck there to start with.'

Tone

This is so important because it gives off many meta-communication signals that go way beyond what the words themselves are actually saying. Take this example: you need to tell your mother/friend/sister/wife that you can't attend a key birthday celebration. If you say, 'I need to talk to you about Joe's birthday dinner . . . ' in a tone that is hesitant, pleading, uncertain or placatory, then you immediately open up the way for being persuaded, guilt-tripped, shamed or manipulated into changing your mind. Now try saying it with belief and certainty in a clear, calm, strong tone. Wouldn't *you* feel much more likely to accept what you are saying? Add in guidelines from the 'Gracious No' (see below) and the chances are that, at best, you can both feel you have got your needs met in a creative problem-solving win–win way; otherwise, you have said what you needed to say without feeling too guilty.

As with all these communication strategies, we get better with practice. So if possible, rehearse by yourself in the mirror beforehand or to a good friend over the phone.

The Gracious No

Most Lovelies particularly struggle with the idea of saying no. I think a sort of phobic response has become entrenched, where we fear saying no, so we avoid saying no, so we have no practice in saying no and a fear of the fear develops.

I have run a workshop exercise in which the participants

walk around the room and every time they encounter someone they have to say 'no' to them – just the word 'no'. The longer they walk around, the more noticeable it is that they are losing their reticence and beginning to enjoy saying no and there is a palpable rise of energy in the room.

You can try this yourself without a workshop. Go somewhere private and stand in front of a mirror. Look yourself clearly and calmly in the eye and say no. Try it in different voices and have some fun. See how it is more effective when you don't smile. This will begin to break your own taboo.

Now, taking this idea a step further, let's look at the components of a successful 'no'. I call this the 'Gracious No', as I think grace is a quality to which many of us aspire. I remember very vividly the first time I noticed someone do this, and it had a lasting and liberating effect on me. I was visiting a friend who was organising the media access to a large sporting event. While he was showing us around the studios and camera positions he took a call on his mobile phone. 'Thank you so much for thinking of us,' I heard him say, very sincerely, 'but I think we'll have to pass on it this time. Good luck with the story.' 'Who was that?' I asked. 'Oh, the *Sun* newspaper,' he said. 'They wanted to come and take some photos on the pitch with page-three girls.' Now there was no way my friend would have wanted his event to be associated with topless models, yet he refused them in such a gracious manner. 'You were so polite,' I said, quizzically. 'Well, manners are free,' he said. 'And you never know when you might need a favour.'

So here's how can you work the Gracious No:

- **Thank the person for asking you** (or 'thinking of you', as my friend said). Nothing more, nothing less. If you're on the phone, take a breath and say this one gracious line first. If you're with them in person, be calm, look them in the eye, don't fidget.

- **Express your refusal in a polite, but clear way.** Keep it short. Purists might say 'Never apologise, never explain', but I think apologising is part of graciousness and therefore important. Copy my friend's line if you like, as it's a good one: 'I'll have to pass on that this time.' If it helps, buy yourself time by *not* deciding on the spot, but saying you must check with your diary/your family or even yourself (something like: 'I don't know yet; I've got to think about what I will be doing this weekend/summer, etc.'). If you do that, it is important that you say when you will get back to them with a decision and stick to it.

- **Try and give a positive follow-on to end on good energy.** If it was about asking for some kind of help, can you suggest someone else who might be able to help them? 'I can't run the cake stall this year, but I think Betty Smith might be interested.' *Don't* suggest someone unless you have a fairly good idea that they might want to do it though, otherwise you are just creating more problems for yourself (when Betty Smith rings up, furious). Or you might throw the possibility forward such as, 'I would love to meet up in a few months when work is less busy'. But again, only say what is true for you, otherwise you will just create future problems. If there are honestly no other options (other people, other dates, etc.), and this may well be the case, then just think of my what my friend said and wish them good luck with the project or say something pleasant like, 'Have a lovely time at the event'.

- *Don't hang around to be persuaded!* This is so important that I have put it in italics and given it a rare exclamation mark. Be it in person or on the phone, end the conversation with speed and grace before the other person smells your guilt and discomfort and tries to change your mind by reason or manipulation.

Jessica the Lovely colleague found the Gracious No particularly useful with demanding colleagues. 'I will say something truthful at the beginning like, "I don't like to say no" or "I hate to appear unhelpful ... *but* I just can't do that as I have a number of other requests." Some people will keep pushing, but a number of more reasonable colleagues realise its true and accept the refusal.'

THE STUCK-RECORD TECHNIQUE

If you are old enough to remember when vinyl records were the only recorded-music format available, you will also probably remember when your favourite records got scratched and the needle of the record player became stuck, playing the same line over and over again. Actually, the same thing happens with CDs, so most of you will have an idea of what I'm getting at with the Stuck-record Technique. Basically, it means that you keep saying the same words over and over to the person to whom you are trying to communicate a clear message. What is really good about it is that it helps you remain calm and not allow yourself to become sidetracked by the highways and byways of red-herring lines of argument.

This is another technique I first learnt at parenting classes. I remember a role play where I was asking my child to put their shoes on as the clock ticked menacingly towards school departure deadline. Standing firm (like a rock), I was told to say very simply and calmly, 'Put your shoes on please, we have to go to school now.' The adult who was playing my son ignored me and carried on playing. 'Put your shoes on please,' I repeated, trying not to alter the volume or tone of my voice. Then I just kept saying, 'shoes' at regular intervals – 'shoes ... shoes ... shoes' – sounding like a stuck record and not getting into that panicky, urgent tone of voice that just seems to up the ante. It worked with my adult role player who put his shoes on, and I felt refreshingly unstressed. Ah ha, I thought, this is all well and good in a role play, but it will never work with a real child. But amazingly, it did. It wasn't 100 per cent every single time, but it was a lot more effective than losing my temper, shouting and ending up late, frazzled and soothing a child who has burst into tears because I've scared them.

Many of my clients have used this technique successfully and say it is really helpful when planning a difficult conversation. But you must watch your tone. Avoid sarcasm, stay gracious, acknowledge what they are saying, but stick to your guns.

Jessica gave me the following example of using the Stuck-record Technique. 'Someone was pushing me to make a decision to fit their agenda, but I said I needed to look into it in more detail, so could I let them know before the end of the week, rather than the end of the day? It was quite funny because I think we both might have been using the "stuck record". For a while she was saying she needed it that day, and I was saying the end of the week. By which point I thought, I am not going to be the one to back down, but didn't want to go round in circles either. So I suggested she went ahead with the rest of the project so as not to cause delays and I would let her know my part by the end of the week. And she agreed. Success!'

I would say that what Jessica used was a combination of Stuck-record Technique plus creative problem-solving, resulting in a win–win compromise. Different communication tools are appropriate for different situations; and the more we dare to experiment the easier it becomes to choose the most appropriate one – be it the small screwdriver or the chainsaw.

Stuck-record part II – fielding difficult responses

The 'shoes … shoes … shoes' example I used earlier seems particularly effective with young children, but with older kids and adults it is obviously more of a two-way interaction because they have the language and logic to argue back, and if you just keep repeating the same phrase you can end up sounding more like a sat-nav system than a calm, assertive human.

Anyone over three years old will often argue back and try to 'win' the situation, as the example above with Jessica shows.

They may use emotional manipulation ('Poor me!' – see Auction of Miseries, page 73), status ('I am more important than you'), shaming ('Other people could manage this') or what Anne Dickson calls 'irrelevant logic'. The trick is then to both acknowledge their responses, but still keep repeating your core message. Try not to get sucked into the *content* of what they are saying and argue against it, but say something like, 'I hear that you are upset/under pressure/only doing what the boss says ... *but* (insert and repeat stuck-record message here).'

This is not as easy as I may be making it sound. But practice will lead quickly to confidence as you gain experience and competence. An almost universal response of clients and workshop attendees (and that includes the Holloway women) to this over the years has been an amazing feeling of empowerment and hope after their first few successes. As I was with the 'shoes' scenario and Jessica with her 'No!', people are amazed and delighted when it works and often wish they had started sooner.

THE FEEDBACK SANDWICH

This is quite widely taught to people whose job involves doing appraisals or assessing work, but others who have not heard of it are usually very pleased to have another helpful communication technique in their tool kit.

Think of the appraisal (or whatever your situation) in terms of a sandwich, where the bread on either side is good, but the filling needs improving. Your bread is the positive statements you make about the person/situation you are dealing with and their skills/performance/qualities, before you ask about the filling: 'How could you do this even better?'

So for example, the client at the beginning of this chapter who wanted to tell HR about her experience of a training day decided to say something like, 'I really appreciate the training you organised for us, thank you. However, it would have been even better if the trainers had researched our area of work more thoroughly: I felt they didn't understand what we do in the field. I hope this feedback helps with your future planning, I can put it in writing if that helps.' This client felt that was the appropriate 'small screwdriver' she needed, along with minimal smiling, some deep breathing beforehand and a calm tone of voice. The chainsaw remained in the shed and she felt encouraged to speak out again.

WHAT WOULD METTE DO?

I have a friend called Mette who I think of as my role model for assertiveness. As you may guess from her name, she comes from Scandinavia – Denmark, to be precise – where I believe there is a cultural norm of straightforward communication. Here is an example of Mette's refreshing straightforwardness.

A few years ago my family went to stay with hers in the summer holidays. Within an hour of our arrival she looked me straight in the eye and said, 'We have just had people staying and I am sick of cooking, so I will not be cooking for you. There are lots of places to eat out and please help yourselves to anything in the kitchen.'

I was, I must admit, shocked by her words. Are women *allowed* to say things like that? I thought in amazement. But as time passed, I realised that we were having a great time, and it was largely because there was a very relaxed atmosphere with no undercurrent of resentment or tension seeping out like poison gas from our hostess. I come from a background where women tend to be what I call high-performance cooks, and feel they have to put on impressive spreads for visitors, all beautifully homemade and handcrafted. But of course, the hard work and pressure behind these show meals comes at a price, and the price is often short tempers and amazing food that is tainted with the aroma of resentment and anger. Not a great taste.

So Mette's honesty was a complete revelation to me. And, of course, it meant we all knew exactly where we stood right from the start, the clarity of which was liberating. I could never be her (although we Marsons believe we are descended from Danish Vikings), but I like to think of her when I am faced with a situation where I want to be more straight-forward, more honest and more clear. What would Mette do? I ask myself. Then I think of the answer, smile and feel a little fear, as it is usually way too far from where I stand in my communication journey for me to be able to copy. But then I think, how could I take just one step towards what Mette would do? This is very helpful, and much more achievable. I picture her with her funky clothes and a cute accent and try and say what I need to say.

Can you think of a Mette figure who you know and like? It doesn't have to be someone you know personally; one of my clients chose Katharine Hepburn in her feisty 1950s' movie persona, while another chose Indiana Jones. Whoever you choose, conjure up their image when you are facing a challenging situation in which you would like to do or say something different from your usual Lovely response. Can you take just one step towards what they might do? What would that look and sound like for you?

CYBER ADVICE – THE LOVELY TEXT AND EMAIL

For some of my clients the majority of their communication is done via email, text and social media like Facebook, and this is where they feel their greatest challenge of assertiveness lies.

When communicating in these ways, the same principles apply, but with none of the meta-communication from body language: be direct, be clear. Think what it is you want to say or ask for, and express it clearly.

A freelance journalist friend of mine decided to cut all flowery waffle, jokes and emoticons from her emails and texts as an experiment – not least because she was fed up with the amount of time and thought it took to compose them. She said she saved lots of time and angst and felt it paid off with an increased respect: 'I became more business-like and others responded in kind. I think my fear was that people needed to like me to give me work, but actually, I just think they want to trust that you are able to do a professional job. I don't think the emoticons really communicate that!'

SUMMARY

In this chapter I have described a number of tools that can help you communicate messages that you find difficult (for example, saying no, complaining, setting boundaries) with more clarity and confidence:

- Be aware of what your body is saying – stand tall and strong. Watch your tone and remember to keep a straight face if you want your message to be taken seriously (this does not make you a horrible person).

- Plan what you are going to say in advance, if possible. Keep it clear and simple; no waffle.

- Remember the 'Gracious No', the 'Stuck-record Technique' and the 'Feedback Sandwich'.

- Ask yourself what your assertive role model would do?

CHAPTER EIGHT

Challenge Your Fear Factor

N ow that you have a set of beautifully polished tools at your disposal, you are ready for the next step: challenging the fears that stop you trying to do something different. I'm going to take you through the process of designing and carrying out your own bespoke behavioural experiments.

Did you ever do experiments as a kid? Maybe you didn't own a junior chemistry set, but you might have mixed rose petals with water to make 'perfume' or soil with water to make sloppy mud pies? Now it's time to re-engage with your inner scientist, and adopt an attitude of open-minded curiosity. Clients love the freedom from self-judgment this brings: as a scientist you are neither right nor wrong; you are simply testing out a hunch, theory or hypothesis, and if it doesn't work, you adjust and try again. It can be playful, creative and fun.

WHAT IS A BEHAVIOURAL EXPERIMENT?

Behavioural experiments are an incredibly powerful vehicle for change. The idea originates with the Behavioural Psychology movement of the 1950s. I mentioned Pavlov's dogs earlier and the idea of a conditioned response (whereby the dogs learnt to associate being fed with the sound of a ringing bell until, quite quickly, their saliva ducts would be activated by the sound of the bell alone, and they would drool even when there was no food in sight).

We humans are no different. If you have had early frightening experiences, your responses become conditioned and you feel fear at just an association with the feared event. As a child, I was terrified of any kind of spider, and they were plentiful on our summer camping holidays, especially in the toilet blocks. As a result, the mere thought of a campsite toilet block or the sighting of a concrete breeze block now makes me anxious.

As discussed in Chapter Two, the behaviour of most Lovelies is disproportionately governed by a fear of anger and disapproval. To avoid these uncomfortable feelings in ourselves, we seek to escape or prevent the situations which may cause them – such as conflict, saying no, not giving people what they want, etc. We often also maximise the behaviours which make us feel safe – by getting people to like us, smoothing over tensions and conflict, agreeing with people, etc. But what happens is that the *prediction* of a feared outcome becomes totally disproportionate to the probability of it happening, and, more important, to our estimate of our ability to handle the feared outcome, even if it does happen.

The idea of a behavioural experiment, therefore, is for you to be able to test your out-of-date hypothesis in a safe, planned and controlled way. This might be something like, 'If I say no to this person, then they will be angry with/not like me and I will not be able to bear their anger/disapproval.' When you test out this prediction, armed with the polished tools and skills we looked at in the last chapter, then you will almost definitely be amazed to realise that even if it does happen, you *can* survive your predicted negative outcome.

We can become trapped by our fear of the fear and the only way out is to make clear these anxious – often child's point-of-view – predictions, and then boldly put them to the test, starting with the smallest and safest. So in line with the theory of Cognitive Behavioural Therapy: change the behaviour and you can change the thoughts and feelings. In my experience, this is the most effective place to begin the process of change, although it rarely feels like the easiest.

OUR HIERARCHY OF FEAR

To overcome a phobia (or 'irrational fear') psychologists often use a technique called systematic desensitisation (also known as Graduated Exposure Therapy).

To begin with, you create a hierarchy of the phobia: what is least feared through to what is most feared. Taking my spider example: at the bottom of my hierarchy, scoring a 1, might be looking at a photograph of a spider, while at the top, scoring a 10, might be holding a big, hairy spider, like a tarantula, in my hand. Using a relaxation technique, such as controlled breathing, I would then 'systematically', and within a time-frame that felt comfortable, work up my hierarchy of fear, exposing myself to my irrational fears and desensitising myself to the stimuli, realising that spiders will not cause me actual harm, and that I can survive the fear. It's a sort of feel-the-fear-and-do-it-anyway approach, though one that predates Susan Jeffers' book of that title.

Compile your own hierarchy of fear

I invite you now to compile your own hierarchy of fear around Lovely behaviours that are problematic to you, where one is the easiest and ten is the hardest or most frightening to you (you don't have to fill in every number from one to ten). Obviously, this is completely personal; don't allow yourself to feel ashamed or foolish because you know others for whom the things you fear would not be a problem. We are all indi-viduals and a complex interaction of our DNA with our experiences gives each of us a unique set of fears. There is no universal hierarchy of fear, just as there is none for emotional pain.

Here is my own hierarchy of fear from a few years ago when I started seriously applying myself to this work:

1 Asking partner for help and support

3 Asking friends for help and support

4 Saying no to people I don't know personally

5   Saying no to friends

7   Public/group disagreement/conflict (for example in a shop, at book club)

9   Saying no to difficult friends

10 Being 'real' in the company of others (for example grumpy, sad, angry) and saying when they've hurt my feelings

Jessica the Lovely colleague devised one for herself at the beginning of our therapy:

1   Not to say 'sorry' when someone bumps into me on the tube

2   Ask somebody to repeat something I didn't hear

3   Say 'excuse me' loudly when someone's in my way, instead of squeezing past

4   Ask people to move down the carriage on the tube

5   Take my time to put my wallet away having paid in a shop (i.e. hold the queue up)

6   Ask a question in a small team meeting

7   Not to say 'sorry' when something is not my fault at work

8   Say 'later' to a request at work

9   Delegate without apologising

10 Say 'no' to a request at work

The next stage is to design an experiment to test out your prediction that something bad and unbearable will happen if you actually carry out one of your feared behaviours. The experiment will help you to gather evidence to prove that the event is perhaps not as scary as you thought it would be – but that *you can survive the fear*, even if it is. Start with something near the bottom of your hierarchy.

Here is a template to help you:

- Describe your experiment

- What is your fantasy prediction/image?

- Current Fear Factor

- More realistic prediction

- What skills and resources can you use?

- Revised Fear Factor

Then afterwards:

- Outcome

- Fear Factor now?

- What have you learnt for your next experiment?

The great thing about describing the fantasy prediction is that it has often acquired epic, filmic proportions and can be more than faintly ludicrous. By bringing it into clear consciousness in this way you can see how extreme it is, and how it possibly belongs to another time in your history – maybe when you were a small and powerless child and an adult's unpredictable outburst of anger or shaming *was* terrifying. As my friend and CBT therapist Nathalie would say, 'It is possible, but is it *likely*?' You can use this question to think of a more realistic prediction, and bring the Fear-Factor rating down a bit. I will illustrate this first with my own example.

My dress experiment

If you look at my hierarchy of fear, taking an item back to a shop rates as a 7. So for the purposes of this book, I decided that I would experiment with this fear and record all the thoughts, feelings and behaviour that went with addressing it.

First I will set the scene. I had bought quite an expensive summer dress from a small boutique-type shop. It is one of those places that sends you a beautiful catalogue through the post, so that you may spend endless hours gazing at the young, flawless models in amazing settings, thinking, probably subliminally, that if you owned one of those silk dresses or cashmere cardigans, then you would be loved and happy and problem-free.

My rational brain knows that this is how advertising works – we link buying stuff with achieving emotional desires. But even with this knowledge, the emotional tug can still be powerful, especially if you are feeling a bit overweight, unattractive and unconfident, as I was on the day I went to this particular shop. So I had probably gone to the shop seeking appearance-based redemption (see the Arc of Redemption myth, page 97), rather than a specific garment, and the sales assistant picked up on that imprecise longing and started, with quite a gushing, persuasive manner, putting dresses in the changing room for me to try on. Half an hour later, I emerged with a poshly wrapped parcel the contents of which I already knew did not really suit me and that I would not wear much, if at all.

I took the dress home, tried it on again, then knew I had to bite the bullet and take it back. Now I hear some of you, even seasoned Lovelies, snigger a little here, as this is not something you would find at all difficult. I know many people's shopping tactic these days is to buy armfuls of clothes, take them home, try them on, then take back all the ones they don't want. Maybe if I did that on a regular basis the idea of taking back a single purchase to a single shop would not be so daunting; but I don't do the former, so the latter *is* daunting.

At this point, my critical voices were already warming up: 'You are so pathetic. Why didn't you stand up to that sales girl?' and 'You are so careless with money; you have made a stupid mistake and now you will have to suffer the consequences and not buy any more new summer clothes.' Wow – don't they sound abusive when written down? Especially that last one which is not only critical, but shaming and punishing: I must be penalised for my mistake by not buying any more summer clothes!

Moving on with the experiment, however, this is how I filled out the form:

- **Describe your experiment:** to go to the shop and ask for a refund.

- **What is your fantasy prediction/image?:** that the shop assistant will be angry with me and try – in a nasty, undermining, critical way – to persuade me to keep it. She will either a) be ice cold and humiliatingly critical in front of customers and staff in a packed shop, saying something like, 'Well, madam, I think you'll find at your age (weight/shape) nothing is going to look any better,' or b) shout and scream at me and possibly physically attack me – again in front of a packed crowd of onlookers.

- **Current Fear Factor:** 7

- **More realistic prediction:** the shop assistant may be cross, but I can be out of the shop quickly and I need never see her again. And if she is really difficult I can ask to see the manager. I have the right to return this item within fourteen days.

- **What skills and resources can you use?** I can slow my breathing down to counteract the fight-or-flight symptoms in my body (see page 62). I can use the Stuck-record Technique.

- **Revised Fear Factor:** 5

- **Outcome:** I waited for a day when I had the time and was feeling reasonably confident. I went into the shop. My stomach was doing somersaults. The same assistant came over. And she *was* really pissed off when I told her I was

returning the dress. I could tell because her previous gushing friendliness had been replaced with a fake smile and
cold, hard eyes. So my prediction was right then – up to a
point. I think it is the kind of shop where the assistants are
on commission for every garment sold, so returns do
matter to them, and I had picked up on that before. As she
was giving me what Paddington Bear called his 'special
stare', I could feel the fear in my body. But I purposefully
took some deep, slow breaths, following the course of the
air through my body with my mind's eye (see breathing
exercise, page 184). I also said to myself, 'This will be over
soon and you need never see this person again. It does not
matter if she hates you now; she can do nothing to harm
you.' That was really helpful. First, it removed me slightly
from feeling caught up in the emotional intensity of the
moment and second, the soothing self-talk made me feel
calmer and safer (see also page 112).

The result was that I got a refund and I got out of the
shop in one piece and not humiliated – in fact, I felt elated.

- **Fear Factor now: 2**

- **What have you learnt for your next experiment?**: I learnt
  to be prepared for the possibility that shop assistants may
  not be calm when confronted with a request to return
  goods, that they may be angry and sarcastic and shaming,
  but that *I could handle that if it happened,* that it wouldn't
  be the end of the world and that *I would survive.*
  Following my experience of returning the dress, I was so
  encouraged that I went on to take two other things back

the same week (a dictaphone, two months past the refund deadline and an ill-fitting bra that I had bought six months before and no longer had the receipt for). As it happens, both interactions were surprisingly simple and straight-forward and the sales staff were understanding, calm and reasonable. In classic systematic desensitisation terms, I could now hold the spider in my hand. Maybe not the tarantula just yet, but a small money spider, which was progress indeed.

Triage your experiments: what is most important *now*?

If you go to the Accident & Emergency ward of a hospital you will usually first be seen by a triage nurse. Their job is to assess how important – literally, how life-threatening – each patient's injury or illness is, and to create a priority list of who should be dealt with first. This can be a helpful way of thinking about the behavioural experiments you would like to do: what is most pressing, *at this moment in time*, to change? Ask yourself what causes you the most disquiet, keeps you awake at night, weighs most heavily on you? Another important question to ask is: what will I gain the most from? Some things feel really difficult to do, yet you would probably gain very little from attempting to change them at the moment. In other words, the cost is probably greater than the gain. Don't let this become another should, or else you may be setting yourself up to fail and feel worse about yourself.

It might be helpful to write a pros-and-cons list to help you gain some clarity. For example, Alison, a delightful workshop participant, wanted to write a letter to her mother as her behavioural experiment. She wanted to explain why she felt so hurt by her judgments and criticisms, which had been going on all Alison's life. This felt horrendously difficult and scary for her to do, and on contemplation of the possible gains and losses, she realised that it was actually quite a risky experiment. Her mother was unlikely to be in a place to hear this feedback, and so might easily throw it back at her in a defensive and critical manner, which could make her feel even worse and put them in a stalemate situation. I explained about the Arc of Redemption (see page 97) and said this triggered my 'arc-of-redemption alert': it was very likely that her mother would never change, unless she experienced a life-changing event or went to therapy (or probably both).

Alison then thought some more and came up with another problem which felt safer to experiment with, yet was actually more pressing in practical terms. She needed to ask former clients for testimonials for her new website. This made her anxious, so she had put off contacting them. What was her fantasy prediction/image? She thought, and then laughed: 'That they will all be ringing each other up, saying things like, "How dare she ask us? What a cheek! And she is so crap at what she does, I can't possibly think of anything positive to say about her!"' Describing her fantasy image immediately allowed Alison to see the comic absurdity of it. 'How likely is that?' asked another participant, kindly. 'Might they not be pleased to help you, if you have helped them?' 'I suppose so,' said Alison, looking unconvinced. 'I would usually be happy to give someone a testimonial, especially if they were very clear about what they needed, that would be very helpful.' 'And what is the Fear Factor?' I asked. 'About a seven,' she said.

Alison decided to devise an experiment whereby she would write a very clear email, detailing exactly what she needed, but with an opt-out clause that allowed people to decline if they were too busy. 'That will save me from feeling rejected if they say no!' she observed wryly. 'Fear Factor now?' asked the group. 'It has gone down to about a three,' she said. 'I will let you know how I get on.'

Alison got in touch a week later to say she had emailed three people and they had all immediately sent back glowing testimonials. 'I think setting the goal in your workshop and being witnessed and supported by the group, made me take the action, which I might have otherwise carried on avoiding,' she said. 'I feel affirmed by my own actions, which is a really positive thing and will encourage me to try more.'

Jessica begins to experiment ...

When I first met Jessica the Lovely colleague, we discussed the idea of her being '1 per cent less lovely' as an immediate experiment (see page 50). She chose to try and not apologise when someone bumped in to her on the tube. The next week, emboldened by the success of that experience ('They didn't even notice. It was the critical voice inside my own head saying, "Where are your manners, young lady?" which I

identified as my aunt, and could answer back to'), we com-
piled a graduated list of experiments for Jessica to try at her
own pace, the highest being saying no to a request at work.

Jessica was very motivated and courageous and started
working through her list, each success encouraging her to move
up her hierarchy of fear (see page 141). Here is an extract from
her therapy journal, taken from near the beginning:

> The calm, patient, witty and intelligent person I've
> always wanted to become – it's not going to happen
> overnight. Maybe assertiveness is the key. If I'm assertive,
> I could be calm because I could ask for what I want, and
> I'd believe I deserve it. If I believe I'm the best person I
> can be, there's no reason to be impatient.
>
> And if I could be relaxed and calm, I could be witty
> instead of babbling and embarrassed. I just need that
> calm feeling inside which would allow me to ask for
> things without sounding apologetic. Does this come first,
> or does it come with practice? Well, if it's practice, then
> I know where to start.

Jessica's successes with being more assertive at work led to
surprising changes that she had not even put on her list: she
managed to set clearer boundaries with her flatmate, she
took on a new and more challenging role at work, she took
up new and daring hobbies and started to make new friends.
It wasn't all straightforward and easy, by any means. Jessica
had setbacks and struggles and there were times when she
almost gave up trying to change in total exasperation. But by

taking things slowly and gently, one small step at a time, she continued her challenge. You can read more feedback from Jessica in Chapters Nine and Eleven.

... so does Liz

We met Liz the Lovely friend in Chapter Three when she had travelled hundreds of miles to have a two-hour therapy session that 'felt like going to a spa', it was so rare to do something just for herself. She left that afternoon with an energised commitment to start setting herself behavioural experiments, especially in the area of 'disappointing others and looking after herself more'.

The first was to be that very evening, when she would tell a friend that she didn't want to go to her poetry reading event as really she wanted to have a nice, long soak in the bath and eat supper with her children. This seemed really scary, but not impossible to Liz, who I encouraged to access her brave side, which clearly existed in many situations past and present. A month later she sent me an email: 'I felt as though someone had switched the light on after my session,' she wrote. 'Exploring where my fear of being told off comes from was hugely helpful. Remembering how badly my dad reacted when I asserted myself as a teenager made me recognise why I am still so keen to please people today.'

Regarding her first behavioural experiment, Liz said she had felt bad doing it, but had texted the friend to say sorry she couldn't make it to the poetry reading and the friend had seemed completely fine about it. 'The funny thing was that friend who I tried my first cancellation on … she said to me that she couldn't believe I was worried about letting her down, as she would never think that of me as I was such a good friend. She knew if I had to cry off then it would be for a good reason, not some casual whim. We actually had a good laugh about it, as that was so far from my fearful prediction that she would be furious and never want to see me again.'

Liz began experimenting with trying to put her own needs before those of others, but she also reported back that she had behaved differently at work with a woman who she felt bullied by. 'I usually just attend the meeting and say nothing and try to be invisible,' she said. 'But this time I got there early and was really friendly towards her. She was a bit surprised, but responded positively. During the meeting I just spoke out when I had something to say. I felt very empowered and that I was being true to myself. All the time I kept saying to myself "What's the worse that can happen?" and "It doesn't matter if she doesn't like me; I don't need her to like me, I just need to find a way to work with her."'

You can find out more about how Liz managed to cut down her social commitments and create more time for what really mattered to her in Chapter Nine.

CREATIVE BRAINSTORM
WITHOUT JUDGMENT

Liz tried doing something different – and it was surprisingly effective. But sometimes it feels impossible to think of potentially different ways to do things, as we are so stuck in our habitual patterns of thought and behaviour.

The creative brainstorm without judgment is a technique that really helps free up your thinking and allows you to come up with new ideas. Write the problem at the top of a piece of paper. Then underneath, write down anything that comes to mind about how to solve the problem. Let your creativity run wild and write down every idea with *no judgment*. This is important because it allows previously unthought-of ideas and potential solutions to slip past the ever-watchful critical voices (see Chapter Five). For example, if you were doing this with a child who had a problem with their teacher and came up with ideas like, 'Put him on a rocket to the moon' or 'Get him kidnapped by pirates', then you'd just calmly write these ideas down, look at them together and decide which options seem best to try. You can also rate all the ideas out of ten if this helps you to gain clarity.

Here's how the creative-brainstorm technique helped Ella, who we first met in Chapter Two.

Ella's flatmate from (imagined) hell

Ella was worried because she had finally found a new flatmate after the last occupant had left following a prolonged sulky silence. She was terrified that things would also go wrong with this new woman and she would be trapped in another embarrassing, awkward dénouement, which would leave her feeling guilty and anxious about the rent. It also reactivated her teenage beliefs that 'I do not fit in; girls do not like me; I will never have any friends'.

I asked Ella to tell me a bit about the new flatmate. 'Well, she seems very nice, quiet, hardworking, respectful of the fact that I need a lot of peace and quiet to study. But so did Frankie at first ...' I then asked her to share with me her fantasy image of what might happen, even if it seemed ludicrous. She thought for a while: 'Well, she told me she has a kind of on-off boyfriend so I suppose it's something like that they will be snogging on the sofa while I'm trying to study or, much, *much* worse ...' She paused here, as if unable to share with me the horror that was unfolding in her mind's eye, '... having very noisy sex in her bedroom all night, keeping me awake and making me feel lonely and inadequate because a) I haven't got a boyfriend and b) I am too inhibited to make that kind of noise.' She looked at me wide-eyed, as if uncertain where that had come from. 'And', I added from my own personal store of flat-share horror stories, 'he will spend hours in your bathroom doing noisy man stuff, then wander around your flat with just a small towel wrapped around his waist.' We burst out laughing. 'How likely do you think that is?' I asked. 'And, more importantly, what could you do *now*, to put your mind at rest, before anything difficult happens?'

Ella looked at me blankly. She admitted that in her mind there was nothing between feeling trapped and helpless in Lovely politeness and waiting for the inevitable terrible fallout which would mean conflict and distress.

'Ok, let's try a creative brainstorm without judgment,' I

offered. Now I have yet to meet a person who doesn't like the sound of this. I think it is the words 'creative' and 'without judgment' – they are such good, positive words that immediately make us feel safe and get the energy flowing. With Ella, she thought of things like: go to the library to study if she brings people home to the flat, and go and stay with friends if she has her boyfriend over. I suggested talking to the new flatmate and maybe deciding some ground rules together that seemed reasonable, like: boyfriends only allowed to stay at weekends.

Ella was amazed. 'I honestly never thought of that, but actually it's perfectly reasonable isn't it?' The process then unlocked the creative problem-solving part of her brain to think of many other possible strategies. 'You are merely transferring your considerable skills,' I said. 'At work you are an amazing problem-solver, but with the flatmate, probably for historical reasons, you couldn't access those skills. You were stuck in trauma, fear and panic, which tend to block our creative problem-solving ability.'

Two weeks later, Ella reported back that she had had a really calm, easy chat with her new flatmate who had agreed to all of her suggestions without a hint of tension. 'I can't believe it was so simple,' said Ella. And these are words I hear often as people begin to experiment with doing something different. When you finally dare to have that difficult conversation, it is usually (though not always) far simpler and less stressful than you had imagined.

SAMANTHA EXPERIMENTS WITH
BEING LESS PERFECT

Some people decide that their most important experiments are to try doing *less* of a certain behaviour, rather than something *different*. If you think back to the childhood patterns we looked at in Chapter Two, some Lovelies are driven by the avoidance of anger, others by what can become an addiction to the approval of others and many by a complex combination of the two.

Samantha, who we met in Chapter Two, decided she wanted to try and experiment with doing *less* to gain the approval of others, and see if she could survive this. As a young girl, Samantha loved pleasing her hard-to-please ballet teacher. Then, as an adult, she transferred all this approval-seeking on to her boss, with long, hard hours of work and responsibility-taking. Now, on maternity leave, she was in the process of transferring it on to her husband and baby. Except, they didn't ask her to, so they weren't that grateful. Her husband wanted her to be her old fun self, but she was exhausted and cross from trying to be the perfect wife and mother, including ironing those endless Babygros and wearing full make-up every day.

Together, we unearthed the main personal rule that under-pinned these behaviours. It was: I MUST ALWAYS TRY MY HARDEST, OTHERWISE PEOPLE WILL THINK THAT I HAVEN'T MADE AN EFFORT. But as we shone a light of inquiry on to this rule, Samantha realised that it was someone else's agenda, most probably her 'amazingly pushy' dance teacher, who needed her to be the perfect ballerina. 'If I achieved this vision of perfection, I don't think my husband would actually want to spend time with me! He doesn't expect me to be this perfect woman.

'Also, as our daughter gets older, I don't want to give her the same perfectionist hang-ups that I have. I want her to be able to approach me with her problems when she's older and, if she knows I've made a few mistakes myself, I might be more approachable.'

Samantha actively worked towards the idea of being 'good enough', rather than perfect, after that session. Her first experiment was to stop ironing the Babygros, then she progressed to spending more days without wearing make-up. She said she quoted the words 'It's ok to be good enough' to herself all the time to help her put things into perspective.

The behavioural experiments described in this chapter are planned or *proactive*. This is a good place to start, because by planning the experiment, many of the elements can be under your control and therefore you can feel safer. Obviously, nothing can be controlled completely, but you probably have the option *when* you speak to your flatmate, boss or partner and *what* you choose to say to them this time. This, in turn, builds up skills and confidence for when things are outside of your control and you must react on the spot to a difficult person or situation. And as these things can occur at any time (and frequently do), I offer some techniques for coping with such *reactive* situations in Chapter Ten.

SUMMARY

You now have some ideas for how to think about and structure your own experiments to challenge the fearful thinking that keeps you trapped in unhelpful ways of doing (or not doing) things:

- Compile your own hierarchy of fear, rating situations from 1 (least scary) to 10 (most scary).

- Design a behavioural experiment around one of your situations; pick something near the bottom of your scale and fill out the template on page 142 to help you plan and prepare for your worst-case outcome.

- Think of relevant tools from Chapter Seven that you might use in your experiment.

- Reward yourself, feel empowered and plan the next experiment.

- Try a creative brainstorm without judgment to get new ideas and options.

CHAPTER NINE

Advanced Behavioural Experiments: Dare to Disappoint

Whenever I mention this idea to someone their eyes widen in slight shock and amazement, and then they smile. It is a you-must-be-joking-because-that-is-*so*-ludicrous smile of relief. But there is more than a grain of an important idea here – it is a great thing even to just think about and it helps us to give ourselves more options.

Why is this such a terrifying idea to the Lovely? What is the Rigid Personal Rule underlying it? I MUST NEVER LET ANYONE DOWN OR ELSE ... Or else what? What is the fear that keeps us trapped in this exhausting, draining way of living? That means we *always* support friends by going to their birthday drinks, dinners, parties, gatherings, poetry readings, art exhibitions, fundraisers, plays, kids' plays, kids' birthdays, parents' funerals ... feel free to add anything of your own – the list is endless. And the thing is, it's not just the events of *close* friends that we support despite illness, overwork and exhaustion; that would, of course, be (mostly) a reasonable thing to do. No, one of the little secrets of Lovelies is that because we can't say no and because we will always make an effort and chat to oddball friends, smooth things over, laugh at the stories and jokes of deluded relatives or entertain the troops with our own stories, that we tend to *also* end up at the parties and events of people we are really not that close to, or sometimes (whisper it) don't even like that much, are a bit scared of or feel sorry for (or all three). Are you nodding your head in agreement? Thought so. But believe it or not, there *are* people out there who when asked to the temporary receptionist's birthday drinks just say, 'Sorry, I would love to, but I really can't make it,' with a gracious smile and no guilt.

How do they do that? Well, you can too. You will need to go back to Chapter Seven to acquire some of the practical skills you need for the task ahead – but first, I think it is helpful to look at the thinking patterns that make the idea of disappointing others so challenging.

LETTING DOWN VERSUS DISAPPOINTING

I was once telling my supervisor, Lynne, that I felt overwhelmed by the number of new clients in my therapy practice. In her usual no-nonsense manner, Lynne asked, 'So why did you take them all on?' Wasn't it obvious, I thought? We are in the *helping* profession. 'I didn't want to let them down,' I said, with the slight defensiveness of tone that creeps in when you know that this may be not the right answer. 'Is there a difference between letting someone down and disappointing them?' Lynne asked. What an amazing question, I thought, having never before considered it. I imagine I looked blank. 'Aren't they the same?' I stumbled, 'If someone is disappointed, then you have let them down, surely?'

'Well,' Lynne answered, 'if you had come all this way today and I had not been here because of a crisis, then you would have been disappointed, but I would not have intentionally let you down – because the circumstances were outside of my control. But if I had simply not turned up, then I would have let you down.' This was so new to me that I could not begin to get my head around it. 'So, if I say no to potential new clients then they might feel disappointed, but I am not necessarily letting them down?' 'Well, you can recommend other therapists who you trust, so they will still probably get the help they need. And who knows, you may ultimately let them down by being too overstretched to give them what they need. If someone feels disappointed, that is their emotion to deal with, not your responsibility. You are not responsible for other people's emotions.'

OVER-EMPATHISING

There are numerous reasons for not being able to say no to other people's requests and demands. As discussed in Chapter

Two, these basically come down to versions of Anger Avoid-ance and Approval Addiction: fear of conflict and a desire to keep the peace at all costs, fear of anger (your own and other people's) and wanting to feel good about ourselves and keep people liking us.

But there is also an empathy angle – we don't want to disappoint others because we know how it feels to be disap-pointed. Therefore we feel a huge amount of guilt that we may be responsible for someone else's hurt feelings.

To avoid the guilt, we often say yes when we really want to say no. But do we really *know* how others will feel in any given situation? We think we do, but we can never actually know. We can only guess and make assumptions, which are actually often based on thinking how *we* would react in that situation – a concept that psychotherapists call 'projection' (like projecting our own movie on to someone else's screen). This is often not at all accurate as a gauge, however, because our movie is chock-a-block with all our history, experience, fears and pain.

So for example, if I had to make someone redundant I would dread it, as I would think it was the worst thing that could happen. I would easily conjure up a terrible vision of them sitting in front of a house-for-sale sign with kids wrapped in rags and a begging bowl. Whereas my friend the executive would think she was giving them the chance to fulfil a lifelong ambition such as sailing around the world or retraining as a circus performer. She would see it as an opportunity; I would see it as a tragedy. Which of us would be right?

Probably neither – because each person will have a unique

reaction to any event. So we need to question how we imagine someone will react when we say no or cancel on them. What happens when friends cancel on us? Often, we are relieved, however fond of them we are, because we wanted an early night. So why might it not be the same for them? Try to not assume you know their emotional reaction. The bottom line is you are not responsible for their reaction; you can only be responsible for your own. This does not mean you will turn into an amoral psychopath, with no empathy for your fellow humans though. Just try experimenting with turning your empathy down a notch or two and see what happens. That is all I am suggesting.

OVERBOOKING

Of course, paradoxically, Lovelies often *do* end up letting people down because they overbook themselves, precisely because they can't say no at the time. In order to avoid letting anyone down, we struggle to say no, thus occasionally (or frequently) becoming overbooked, double-booked, triple-booked and much more besides.

Does this happen to you? Do you end up with a Friday evening scribbled in many different pens in your diary that reads something like this:

Help with class tea at school. Pop in to X's leaving drinks. Cook dinner for family. Meet Y for cinema. Try and pop in to say hello at Z's birthday party.

You end up doing all of them unsatisfactorily (even the cinema is slightly spoiled by wondering how long the ads will run, what time will it end, how long will Y want to discuss the film for, when you can politely leave, how long it will take to find Z's party venue . . .), some of them guiltily (you had to rush through the family dinner and didn't catch up with your kids properly as you'd wanted to, and only made it to the party for a few minutes as your babysitter had to get home) or none of them at all as you had similarly overbooked yourself on Tuesday, Wednesday and Thursday and have collapsed into bed ill and exhausted by Friday afternoon. Sound familiar?

So what is the answer? Again, it's daring to experiment with doing things a bit differently.

DISAPPOINT SOMEONE DAILY

Dare to test out your hidden prediction that there will be anger, disapproval and friends storming out of your life in disgust leaving you friendless and uninvited, rather than feeling popular, in demand and busy, but sometimes – often? – overstretched, exhausted and resentful.

Kirsty's week of disappointing others

Kirsty volunteered to try and do this Advanced Behavioural Experiment for one week and agreed to share the diary of her attempts (names have been changed):

Wednesday I had managed to triple-book tonight because I didn't want to let anyone down and was a coward. Was supposed to be meeting Sean, old uni friend who is stuck at home with the kids and rarely gets the chance to go out, go to the pictures with Marie, who I haven't seen for ages and feel a bit guilty about, and then Paul reminded me that I was going to his work event the same night! Knew of problem for about a week, but put off contacting M and S because felt guilty, thus compounding the guilt and self-beating every day about why hadn't I rung them yet ... So cost myself lots of angst and stress because of fear of disappointing them. In the end emailed them both – coward's way out. They were fine about it, but probably would have been even finer if they had had even more notice. Must be brave and give people more notice! These two are easy because they are both a bit Lovely and wouldn't complain.

Thursday Supposed to go out tonight to meet scary Babs, who's down for work. But as day went on, realised I was knackered and needed an early night because of late night and too much booze at work do, and Max waking me at six. Before, there is no way that I would have even *thought* of cancelling. I would have done something to revive myself like eat chocolate or have a shower and then just gone. And, once there, I would not have mentioned that I was tired, and gone into lively, entertaining mode – or whatever was required.

But being in week of 'disappointing someone daily', decided to bite the bullet and seize opportunity to do something different. My Fear Factor was quite high, as this friend is a person who, in the past, has expressed her disappointment in no uncertain terms. Does a good line in angry silence which registers very highly on my sensitive rage-o-meter. Was SO scared, left it till 5pm to call. Did some deep breathing and rehearsed my line. Stomach going crazy and hand shaking. Amazingly, it went to voicemail! Such relief! Left my message. Didn't lie and make an excuse. Said I was too tired and wanted an early night. Also said hoped she wouldn't be too disappointed, but knew other friends were meeting her. In state of fear, waiting for her angry call back. Couldn't focus on bedtime story. Sent text in case didn't get my message. Finally, she called and was ... sweetness and light! Said no worries, get your early night, we'll meet soon. Couldn't believe it! My bravest experiment to date! Can't believe didn't try it earlier. Feel very emboldened to do more.

Friday Gave 'Gracious No' to estate agent who was a bit frosty, but later sent nice email. My fault as had been too enthusiastic about unsuitable flat cos didn't want to hurt his feelings. Bonkers behaviour – Paul is completely straight about these things. Do I care if the estate agent doesn't like me? Think I secretly want to be one of his favourites ...

Saturday Difficult client at beauty rooms. Didn't tell her what she wanted to hear, she wanted extra time, but I had to stick to boundaries – a real struggle for me. She started telling me sad story about her break-up as she was about to leave, so I was really torn. Felt mean and cruel, but stuck to my boundaries (invoked name of boss to help).

Sunday Said no to the cat! Can't resist the manipulation when she comes looking for a stroke: the big eyes, the pitiful meowing. I always thought I cannot reject the cat; she will feel so sad and unwanted. But I am allergic to cat fur, so even one stroke makes my eyes red and itchy, my throat tight and scratchy ten minutes later, so put my needs ahead of hers and ignored her. Anyway, how do I know what the cat is thinking and feeling? Jacqui would say I was projecting my inner rejected child on to the cat!

Paul's mum came for lunch. Tried not to be the perfect daughter-in-law and left attention-giving to him. When she started talking about family Xmas plans I said we didn't know what we were doing yet and would get back to her. She looked majorly pissed off cos I usually agree to everything. Felt awkward. Hardest reaction yet.

Monday Starting new sleep regime with Max. Setting clearer boundaries with bedtime and when he comes into our bed take him back into his own, kindly but firmly. The book says this will break the habit in fourteen days. Hope so, as it is really tough on us all. Max cried for over an hour which ripped my heart out. Paul is on side, so that will help.

Tuesday Boiler broke again! Feel let down by plumber, even though have devoted hours of time and tea building relationship with him so he would treat us well. Was a bit off with him on the phone and told the truth – we are freezing! Marie said buy boiler insurance, then you know where you stand and don't have to waste energy being charming.

I asked Kirsty how she felt after her week. 'It was amazing to realise kind of what I can get away with. People cared far less than I imagined and were much more reasonable. Some of it felt a bit fluffy, but I tell you, that early night I gained allowed me the strength and energy to start trying to sleep-train Max, which I think could make a massive difference to my sanity!' What was the most difficult part? I asked. 'Definitely my mother-in-law. She was shocked, I think, at me not being my usual doormat self. It was a bit strained after that – I think she was actually furious with me.'

Kirsty and I agreed that there would certainly be more chal-lenges ahead for her as she decided to stick with not always putting the needs of others first.

PREPARE FOR CHANGE BACK!

What Kirsty encountered with her mother-in-law was the Change Back! phenomenon so well documented by Harriet Lerner in her classic book *The Dance of Anger*. You are changing the rules by doing something different, and the people around you – who you have inadvertently trained to expect certain things from you – will, almost definitely, be disappointed. Some will be hurt and angry and will express this in no uncertain terms (like Kirsty's son) and others more indirectly (like her mother-in-law). Still others will disappear from your life when they realise that the old rules of engagement seem to have changed and they do not want to play by the new ones. All of them will probably let you know how they feel in one way or another. And that is the Change Back! phenomenon.

You, of course, will be so hyper-vigilant to the merest whiff of these emotions that you have spent your whole life trying to avoid, that they don't actually need to say anything – the slightest hint of a downturned mouth or narrowed eye will most likely send your brain's threat detector – the amygdala – into frenzied overdrive (see 'The tiger in the mind', page 181). When this almost inevitably happens, try and remind yourself *why* you wanted to change in the first place – what was your motivation? In the words made famous by the civil rights movement: keep your eyes on the prize. It may be that you want to be a role model for your children (as Samantha identified – see page 157) or realise that this is an important path to better health and wellbeing (as Amanda discovered – see page 45).

Try not to waver on your newly assertive behaviour as this will send mixed messages and allow people (especially children) to doubt what you say. Their Change Back! behaviour might include manipulation, guilt-tripping or punishment, such as sulking or withdrawing love and affection. Enlist the support of a trusted friend to try and stay firm, especially if the goal is dear to you. And sometimes it is a good idea to explain to your loved ones in a calm and clear way *why* you are changing the rules and how it might be best for everyone. If you believe in your own rationale, and that you have the right to do what you are trying to do, then chances are you can convince them too.

LIZ'S PROGRESS

Liz the Lovely friend you first met in Chapter Three, had been experimenting with disappointing people for over a year when I contacted her to see how it was going. She wrote in an email:

I absolutely feel that lots of things have changed as a result of my therapy. Generally, I think I'm calmer and much less stressy than I used to be. Although I haven't removed stress completely from my life, I deal with it better now. I realised that I felt a sense of duty to see all my friends regularly and I was able to question that. I had a right good 'clear-out' where my friends were concerned. The ones that remain are a pleasure and have made me happier, but this has been a long and hard journey. I have a few close friends now and it suits me better. I feel very much more in control of all of my relationships in that I don't find them a pressure or an obligation any more.

But by far the best outcome has been my relationship with my children. This is as close to perfect as I think I'll ever get. I've learnt to let things go and choose my battles carefully. The result has been that we are all closer, we talk lots, spend more time together and their friends spend more time at my house than their own. I do sometimes still feel a bit taken for granted and often count to ten when the house is a mess and chaotic, BUT I would prefer a messy house and a close relationship than the other way round.

Kirsty's and Liz's stories demonstrate bringing about relatively large-scale, obvious disappointments. But what of causing more subtle ones? What would happen if we chose to *not* smile encouragingly, laugh at people's jokes and stories, ask them interested questions and be a good facilitator? I call these micro-disappointments.

PENNY, MEN AND MICRO-DISAPPOINTMENTS

At one of my workshops, the discussion turned to this idea of micro-disappointments and I asked the group to see if they could think of their own examples, to begin to bring awareness to these behaviours. One woman said that she realised she did this, especially with men. 'I don't mean to sound arrogant,' she said, with embarrassment, 'but men often get crushes on me when I don't even *like* them. I think I may have spent my life doing what you are describing, but never fully realising it – and not knowing that there was any other way to be.' Penny, a glamorous head teacher in her fifties laughed in terrible recognition at this. 'Listen,' she said, bravely sharing with the group, 'I have been married three times because I didn't want to disappoint the men who wanted to marry me.' It is no exaggeration to say that there was an audible gasp from the rest of the group. 'You're joking, aren't you?' asked the woman sitting next to her. 'I wish I were,' Penny replied sheepishly. 'My last husband proposed to me on Valentine's Day in a beautiful restaurant. As he held the ring out, I could see the vulnerability in his eyes, the fear that I might turn him down, and I just couldn't bring myself to say no. I knew, as I was saying yes, that I did not want to marry him and this was not the right thing to do, but I couldn't bear to see the pain and disappointment in his face.' 'Wow,' said her neighbour. 'Are you dating now?' 'Well, I have in fact got a date tonight, with a man who I like, but not enough, and I'm just thinking about whether I could experiment with being less enthusiastic, laughing less at his bad jokes and being a bit cooler – a bit more real. It will be tough though. Old habits die hard.'

We will find out what happened on Penny's date in Chapter Eleven. Meanwhile, here is another Advanced Behavioural Experiment challenge.

HELP LESS – SIT ON YOUR HANDS

Can you experiment with – literally – sitting on your hands and *not* volunteering when there is a need for a volunteer (or sometimes not even an obvious need for a volunteer)? How many Rigid Personal Rules are you breaking by seeing a need and doing ... nothing. Because other people will always have needs, the demand is endless. But what about *your* needs – where do they fit in to this belief?

I was challenged to do this very recently. I was waiting for the number 46 bus and a small drama began to unfold. A woman rushed up looking a bit panicky and started asking people in the queue where the bus was going and when it was due. A minute later I looked up and she and another woman from the queue were standing in the road, wildly trying to wave down a taxi. As I sat on a wooden bench behind the bus stop, sipping my takeaway coffee and enjoying a rare bit of spring sunshine on my pale winter skin (see 'Rate your day', page 101), I felt tension entering my body. I could feel the anxiety of both woman A and woman B as they tried to flag down a vehicle. Their body language was tense and desperate. I began spinning a story around what I could see: woman A needed to get to an urgent appointment, but she was lost and late, and woman B was trying, ineffectually, to help her. I could feel the Lovely neural pathways in my brain lighting up, telling me, *Help them! Get involved!* But instead, I took some deep breaths and asked myself, 'Can I really do any more than they are already doing?'

I mindfully concentrated on physical sensations in the

here and now – the taste of my coffee, the warmth of the sun – to try and calm myself. When I next looked up, woman A had gone, having presumably found a cab or found her own solution. Whatever it was, my help had not been needed.

Don't get involved. *Sit on your hands.*

HOW TO ASK FOR HELP

Usually on the flip side of the beliefs and behaviours illustrated above that lead to over-helping is the huge struggle involved with asking for help for ourselves. I have put this in Advanced Behavioural Experiments because, in many ways, this might be the hardest thing of all for many Lovelies to do. Are you cringing as you read this? Or were you – more likely – about to skip over this section altogether because you don't want to think about it?

Clients talk to me a lot about why they can't ask for help. The common themes are various versions of Rigid Personal Rules, such as: I MUST BE STRONG, SELF-SUFFICIENT AND INVUL-NERABLE AT ALL TIMES. If then asked to think about how they would feel if they did ask for help, then invariably the opposite side of the rule emerges: IF I ASK FOR HELP I WILL BE SEEN AS WEAK, NEEDY AND VULNERABLE; OTHERS MIGHT TAKE ADVANTAGE OF ME AND I WILL BE INDEBTED TO THEM. Other common rules tend to be versions of control and perfectionism, which are usually underpinned by unacknowledged anxiety, for example: there's no point in asking someone to help because they won't do it properly, anyway; it's quicker and simpler just to do it all myself.

This way of thinking, of course, fuels resentment, martyrdom and isolation and the belief: I am all alone with all these responsibilities and there is no one who can help me.

Susie's story

If you remember from Chapter One, Susie was brought up with her five siblings by a widowed mother who worked at three jobs to make ends meet. The unspoken family rule was: never tell anyone your business or ask anyone for help; we stick together and we manage alone. Susie had carried this rule into adulthood, and although she was good at asking her kids to pull their weight (as she and her brothers had done), she rarely confided in anyone and *never* asked others for help, unless she could pay them in some way.

We worked on this for months in our sessions. Susie, a very insightful woman, was quick to see the link between the fact that she felt emotionally isolated as no one knew or understood her and the fact that she didn't share her less-than-strong-and-coping thoughts and feelings with anyone. 'They all think I am this omnipotent Superwoman!' she would complain to me. 'But why do they think that?' I would ask. 'Only you can dare to let them know the truth – that you are a struggling human being like us all.' But this felt way too risky for Susie to contemplate. She knew it was because her inner child was terrified of breaking the family rule; on some level it felt like life or death, but it was hard to persuade her inner child to let her adult self take the plunge.

Encouraged and supported by our work in therapy, Susie did begin taking these important risks. She became close to two other mums and began to reveal aspects of her full self that she had previously kept tightly and secretively locked away. She also asked them for some practical help in picking up her kids one day a week from school, so she could do an adult-education course that was important to her need for expression.

Jessica's progress

Lovely colleague Jessica's family ethic was also one where you soldiered on alone and didn't ask for help. It made her feel exposed and foolish to ask questions at work because she *should* know what to do or be able to work it out herself. But while courageously moving up her hierarchy of fear (see Chapter Eight), Jessica got to the point where she realised she needed to ask her boss for help in setting boundaries and saying no to colleagues who made unreasonable requests. She could not do this alone. Here is an entry from her therapy journal:

> Being really open with my manager was a big step. I actually said that I found it difficult to say no to some of the requests and deadlines that were not very reasonable. That felt quite scary because it was like I was criticising the colleagues who came to us with last-minute requests. But he said he thought I was right! He suggested that I try

pushing back on my own first and that I could always refer back to him if that didn't work. And sometimes, just knowing he was sitting next to me when someone came over with a request actually gave me the confidence to push back on my own.

I asked Jessica how it had felt when it came to the crunch and she started refusing the requests of colleagues. 'I was very nervous at first,' she told me. 'But it became easier with practice. I think people are more used to the possibility of hearing a "no" now.' She smiled. 'You know the biggest surprise? That in most cases the response was that it was fine that I said I couldn't do something!'

Where will this idea take you?

You really don't have to disappoint someone *daily*. And you certainly shouldn't invent disappointments just to be a star pupil and come top of this class. I created the idea to make it memorable, and it seems to bring a spark of playfulness to a set of challenges that can seem insurmountable and terrifying. A friend of mine says she thinks of it often when she is stuck in traffic jams, and it brings a mischievous smile to her lips – because her self-assigned role is to look after people emotionally and keep them all happy, not disappoint them for goodness sake! But she says it gives her a sense of possibility – that things could be different, that she will not be a wicked and evil person if she tries something a little different occasionally. 'I have even begun to not automatically let *every* driver into the queue in front of me!' she said, with a twinkle in her eye.

Remember: just because you start taking more notice and care of your own needs does not make you a bad or selfish person. You will begin to discover that what you do give is given more freely and genuinely and that is better for everyone.

SUMMARY

This chapter looked at further ways to experiment with breaking your old, habitual Lovely patterns of thinking and behaving:

- There is a difference between letting someone down and them being disappointed. You are not responsible for the emotions of others.

- You cannot assume the response of other people. They might be relieved you have cancelled because they wanted an early night.

- Be prepared for the eventuality that people will try, through a variety of challenging direct and indirect communications, to make you change back to your old Curse of Lovely ways. Try and stay firm and focused on why you are changing.

- Help less – sit on your hands and don't rush to volunteer.

- Experiment with sharing your vulnerabilities with trusted people and asking for help, both emotional and practical.

CHAPTER TEN

Be Prepared For the Unexpected

Once you have tried out some behavioural experiments (and even some Advanced Behavioural Experiments) you will hopefully begin to feel more confident and able to deal with difficult situations and people where you have a chance to think through your strategy and put a plan into place. I call this *proactive* behaviour because, to a certain extent, you are in control and driving the interaction. Take my dress-returning experiment (see page 143): I could control the time and the day I did it, thus, theoretically, waiting until I felt strong enough to deal with a fearful situation. I couldn't control how they would respond to me but, having formulated my plan, I had thought through how I would respond to various eventualities, including my fantasy vision of a full-scale physical fight (a bit like a

Hollywood bar-room brawl) and had selected and polished the appropriate tools for the occasion.

EMERGENCY STRATEGIES

Many of our most difficult interactions in life are, of course, *reactive*: they are totally unplanned and unexpected and we are forced to react to other people, and their sometimes powerful emotions, on the spot. Even with unforeseen circumstances though, there are strategies we can use to help us cope.

I want to start with something gentle, yet extremely effective. It is the power of our breath to enable change. That may sound a little simplistic, but I have learnt the transforming power of mindful breathing and I would like to share it with you. Here is an example to illustrate the process.

Recently I was in Holland running a training workshop for staff of many different nationalities. One of the delegates looked sullen and cross, as if she clearly didn't want to be there – would rather be anywhere, in fact, than the airless training room on probably one of the last sunny days of summer. She scowled at me and informed me crossly, in a harsh, unhappy voice, that she would have to sit at the front as she was a bit deaf and that I would have to speak up (I don't think I had even spoken at this point).

After I had delivered the first ten minutes of material, I paused to ask for feedback from the group. Olga, the difficult delegate, barked, 'I couldn't hear a word of it.' 'Ok,' I said,

feeling the cold fingers of fear creep up my body, but plaster-
ing a pleasant smile on my face (which almost definitely did
not reach my eyes). 'Can anyone summarise for Olga what
we've just done?' But before anyone could answer, Olga
jumped in: 'There is no need. I know it all already. Psychology
is my hobby. There is nothing you can teach me.'

I am laughing now as I write this, but at the time I wanted
to burst into tears and run away. Or maybe slap her. Fight,
flight or freeze – the body's physiological responses to perceived
threat (see page 62) – kick in so quickly. My stomach began to
churn with anxiety, my shoulder muscles were setting into
rock-like forms and my mouth was dry. The threat detector
part of my brain, the amygdala, was going crazy in a can't-be-
ignored car-alarm kind of way: 'NAA NAA NAA! Get out of
here! Leave the building at once! Do not pause to collect your
flip chart! This is a threat! You may die!' (As a trainee journalist, I was taught never to use exclamation marks, but I do
think the amygdala speaks to us in frantic exclamations.)

The tiger in the mind

For millions of years, before humans had developed the parts
of the brain that deal with higher cognitive functions such as
thinking, planning and problem-solving, the amygdala worked as
a highly sensitive threat detector to help keep us alive to pass
on our genes. So, for example, if our prehistoric ancestors saw
a distant movement in the savannah that might have suggested

a predator such as a sabre-tooth tiger, the amygdala would be triggered, and what we now call the stress response set into play: adrenalin coursing round the body, heart beating extra fast, pumping blood to the limbs ready to grapple with the tiger (fight), to run for your life (flight) or hide in the grass (freeze).

Clients seem to find it very helpful to know that our stress responses are governed by something over which we have very little control, but which makes perfect sense when thought of in evolutionary terms.

Today, we humans are highly evolved beings with complex cognitive functions. We don't have to be constantly on the look-out for marauding wild animals. But our efficient amygdala is still ever alert to the slightest sign of danger, even though those threats now come mostly in the form of thoughts. They are the tigers in our mind, rather than in the savannah.

In my training workshop, there was no real physical danger with Olga, but I sensed her anger, which immediately triggered my stress response.

Once in the grip of this physiological response, it is almost impossible for us to think calmly and logically, as the amygdala is dominating the brain and the parts responsible for cognitive function are impaired or blocked. 'I can't think straight!' you might yell (or think), and this is often the exact truth. To use the car-alarm metaphor again – when the alarm is triggered, it disables the car-key functions, so no one can get into the car or start up the engine to drive away. In the same way that the car will not start, neither will our thinking brains.

Breath is the key

This is where we come back to the simple but extremely effective idea of the power of our breath. It seems that by consciously focusing on our breath, by taking our attention to the breath going in and out of our bodies, we can break the power of our centuries-old inbuilt car alarm and access the thinking parts of our brain.

Basically, you can approach your noisy, panicking car (NAA, NAA, NAA), take three deep breaths and the key will work again; the door will open, the ignition will turn and you can drive to your destination. This takes a bit of practice, but is amazingly effective. It can seem to last an eternity, but in reality, three low, conscious breaths only last a few seconds and can give you just enough of a break from your tiger-in-the-mind terrors to be able to access the calm, problem-solving parts of your brain.

With Olga, I remembered the power of my breath. I very slowly and consciously breathed in and breathed out. I don't mean I stared down at my stomach, but I became aware of my breath – brought my mind's eye to it, if you like – and felt it push my stomach against the waistband of my trousers as I breathed out deeply. Then I smiled at Olga and realised that behind her frightening, angry-looking face, *she* was probably frightened herself.

According to a concept in psychotherapy, our behaviours

come in reciprocal pairs, so here Olga might be: frightened – frightening. But we can only access our empathy towards a scary person once our amygdala (car alarm) has been switched off, as empathy is a higher brain function that does not work when we are in the grip of the fight-or-flight response. Having switched off the car alarm through deep breathing, I was then able to access my empathetic response. With my experience of working with some clients with hearing difficulties, I realised that this was possibly the source of her anxiety and sought to reassure her that her expertise was very welcome and asked her to help me out if I had overlooked any important points.

Now regardless of what you think of my solution and how yours might have been different, the important point here is that I could access *any* problem-solving ability and move on with a difficult situation. Amazingly, my solution seemed to work a treat and Olga became my honorary assistant and supporter, leading the applause at the end of the workshop.

Breathing exercise

First bring your attention to your breathing. Follow the in- and out-breaths for a few moments. It helps if you can gently place a hand on your stomach to feel it rise and fall. It will expand (rise) with the in-breath and fall back down as you breathe out. Just concentrating on your breathing, without trying to change it, will bring your attention into the present moment and dis-tract you from any unhelpful thoughts that may be swirling around inside your mind, causing you to feel anxiety and tension.

To take this a step further, actively slow down the rate at which you are breathing, by gently lengthening the in-breaths and the out-breaths. It is really helpful to breathe in for a count of three, and breathe out for a count of five. This is called 'three-five breathing' and is very effective at helping you to feel calmer and enabling you to access your clear thinking.

Fear of anger

As we saw in Chapter Two, our fear of anger usually goes back to childhood when we were relatively powerless when confronted with the anger of people around us. As small chil-dren we were dependent on the adults who looked after us, and if their anger caused us harm or frightened us, then there was very little we could do about it. Of the threat responses we have looked at, fighting or running away is not a long-term solution when you are a dependent child, while to 'freeze' is probably the least effective defence. The unpredictable nature of an angry outburst means that a child's 'solution' is often to try and control the one thing they can control – their own behaviour – so as not to 'provoke' the unpredictable person. And so can often begin the pattern of Lovely children who become Lovely adults – hypersensitive to the slightest sign of impending anger in others and experts at controlling – or suppressing – their own anger.

It is important to realise that your fear response is often that of yourself as a small, powerless child and out of all proportion to the current threat and your adult ability to deal with it. Again, it is the amygdala that is responsible for this: it stores old memories of threatening events and has no sense of time. So when, for example, I saw Olga's teeth clench and her eyes narrow, my amygdala car alarm reacted as if I was three years old and about to be slapped. This Toddler Terror (see page 112) lurks behind many of our reactions. We are reacting 'historically' and not in the present.

Anchor yourself

I have found the mindfulness technique of 'anchoring' yourself into the present moment an effective antidote to Toddler Terror. The idea is that you use your senses to bring yourself back to the present, to experience the here and now through touch, taste, smell, hearing and vision. You might feel the ground beneath your feet, for example – literally 'grounding' yourself. Other ideas for anchoring that are popular with my clients include:

- Touching a piece of jewellery they are wearing, especially if it has sentimental significance having been given to them by a loved one, perhaps.

- Feeling the fabric of a piece of clothing they are wearing.

- Smelling their perfume.

- Taking a sip of water.

- Awareness of their breath.

Any of these can work as an anchor to bring you back into the moment.

BEAR – Breathe, Eulogise, Accept, Respect

This technique uses the idea of harnessing the power of your breath to help defuse sudden feelings of fear and takes it a step further, adding guidance to help you disarm the frightening person, so they feel safe and you do not feel attacked.

My colleague Val Sampson and I created the acronym BEAR when we were running workshops based on her book, *Tantra: the Art of Mind-blowing Sex*. We designed it specifically for couples who were in conflict over intimate issues, but found even the thought of conversation too daunting, and so avoided talking about the very subjects that could potentially transform their relationship.

The idea behind 'BEAR' was that in a time of fear and stress the word is easy to remember and you would most likely recall at least what the first two letters stood for, which could be enough to save the moment. Both Val and I have taught BEAR to scores of clients who have used it to help with a vast range of difficult people and conversations, all with very positive results.

B is for breathe

Not only can the breath take us from the grip of adrenalin-coursing fight, flight or freeze to the calmer, more rational thinking parts of the brain, it can also soften the powerful non-verbal signals which we emit when we are anxious. As mentioned earlier, studies consistently show that only a tiny proportion of our communication is understood from the actual words used, as opposed to the tone of voice and, in particular, body language (see page 119). And much of that is from what is called the micro non-verbal communication of the face, especially the eyes. Often, when we know we're going to say something difficult to our partner or we're responding to them saying something that is difficult to hear, we hold a lot of tension in our face because we're anxious, and they pick up on those powerful non-verbal cues. Unhelpfully, many of the facial signs of anxiety are very similar to those for anger: we might have tension in the jaw, which makes it look set and angry, a furrowed brow and our pupils may become tiny pinpricks, making our face look hard, cold and hostile. So our partner (or friend/boss/child/parent/colleague) can easily think we are angry and, within a nanosecond, their amygdala will have subconsciously pro-voked their body into either defensive or attacking behaviour (fight or flight).

If you consciously breathe the tension out of your face before you speak, or reply, then this will really help to soften the non-verbal cues you are transmitting. As you do so, check that you are not clenching your teeth, move your jaw about a bit to loosen the tension and even look in a mirror, if you have the chance, to see what messages your face is giving off. (Most people would be shocked if they were to see a video recording of themselves having a difficult conversation.)

E is for eulogise

Eulogise means 'to praise highly'. The idea is that by saying something *genuinely* complimentary to the difficult person or in the difficult situation, we help them to feel safe and not hostile, defensive or attacking. This isn't about being manipulative, so don't say something that you don't really mean, just to butter them up. They will sense your insincerity and the whole process will backfire. It is also helpful if you can think of something to say that is specific and descriptive, rather than general. For example, it would be better to say to your partner something like, 'I love it when we cuddle up and watch the news at night', rather than 'You know that I love you'.

A is for accept

Accepting is about listening with your full attention, without sighing, interrupting or even raising your eyebrows. Each of you will hold your own truth about any given situation, and tempting as it is to engage in a verbal tug of war – 'See it my way'/'No, you see it my way' – battles like these make serious dents in any relationship, whether at home or at work. Once you accept that another person holds a different truth to you – and that they are perfectly entitled to do so – you can then start to problem-solve in a fruitful and respectful way.

R is for respect

It is amazing how disrespectfully we can speak to those clos-est to us. A favourite is the (literal or metaphorical) finger pointing and accusations starting with the word 'you' – 'You never do X', 'You always say Y', 'You are such a Z' – usually delivered in a tone which probably falls somewhere between unloving and contempt.

Before you open your mouth to speak, ask yourself: am I naming, shaming or blaming this person? And instead, try to put your thoughts into a statement that expresses your feelings starting with 'I'.

Now let me share with you an example that came up at one of our workshops. A woman told us how she had opened a beautifully wrapped present at the beginning of an anniversary weekend away, only to find it contained a tiny PVC dress. She said she felt a huge rush of negative thoughts and feelings towards her husband: how could he have done this? Who did he think she was – that slutty ex of his? Didn't he love her at all? Had she made a terrible mistake? Disappointment, shock, embarrassment, anger, inadequacy and fear were all mixed together.

She expressed her thoughts in no uncertain terms, he shouted back and their romantic weekend was ruined. In the workshop, she thought about what might have been different had she used BEAR.

After breathing (Breathe) to calm the panic, she thought of something genuinely complimentary to say (Eulogise): 'I'm touched that you put thought and effort into buying me a pres-ent and (Accept) I realise this is something you might want to experiment with. But I don't feel comfortable in something so revealing (**R**espectful 'I' statement).'

Using the tools outlined in this chapter seems to help open the way to dialogue and problem-solving together, rather than fighting, where one person is attacking and the other one's being defensive, and off it spirals.

SUMMARY

There are often times when we feel assailed by unexpected confrontation. This chapter has aimed to give you some emergency tools to help cope with these:

- The power of your breath: when someone triggers your fear response, take two or three long, slow breaths to stop your amygdala 'car alarm' and give yourself time to think more calmly and clearly.

- Try 'anchoring' yourself in the present moment when confronted with your fear response: touch/taste/smell/hear/see yourself back to the here and now.

- Remember BEAR – Breathe, Eulogise, Accept, Respect – when you find yourself in a difficult conversation or situation.

CHAPTER ELEVEN

Lovely, With Choice

The main idea of this book is to help you to begin to make changes, so that you can still be Lovely, but when *you* choose to be. Hence: Lovely, with choice. As I have said before, I am not criticising anyone's Lovely behaviours in any way. These are a great set of skills to have and the envy of many of those who struggle to connect with people. I just want to help you gain options, so that other choices of behaviour are available to you, and so that when you do choose to be lovely, it is given from a place of freedom. This will help to stop you feeling trapped by others' expectations of you – in other words free you from the Curse of Lovely and begin turning it into a blessing.

BUT WHO AM I NOW?

If you have had these behaviours for many years, and certainly if they stem from unconscious childhood rules and beliefs, then it can be extremely difficult to change them. Not only will you have the Change Back! pressure from others that we looked at in Chapter Nine, but it can be difficult to know just who you *are* if you are not in default Lovely mode.

Jessica the Lovely colleague told me that she struggled to find what she called her 'new persona'. 'I've never really been an assertive person before,' she said, 'so I'm not sure who she is. I've realised that as I've gained confidence, I've adopted a new way of talking and that this new me sometimes sounds rather patronising.' Another one of my clients also said to me recently, 'It was so much easier when I was just on auto-pilot and pleasing everyone. Now I am trying to be real and authentic, I feel naked and exposed. It's kind of like I don't really know how to behave now; it's making me feel a bit nervous and vulnerable.'

Jessica didn't want to go back to what she saw as the 'always apologetic' person she had been before, so she came up with a bold solution – to ask a couple of trusted colleagues for feedback. 'I said to them, "Can you please tell me when I'm using this patronising new voice to you, which I don't like?" And this helps, as I either see a friendly smirk on their faces when I'm talking, then I stop and rephrase things, or I'll actually catch myself and say, "I'm doing it again, aren't I?" And it's not the end of the world.'

THE HEALTHY FALSE SELF

The psychotherapist who first wrote about the False and True Selves was D. W. Winnicott. His idea was that everyone has this protective outer layer, and he argued that we need a *healthy* False Self which allows us to be polite and well-mannered in public. It is only when we have lost touch with our inner True Selves that we are in trouble (or unhealthy).

As social beings, we can't be our true selves the whole time; we have to take into account the needs of others and the social requirements of each situation. Thus, we might want to tell our boss where to stick their proposal, fling all our clothes off at a stuffy meeting and dance naked on the table or sulk in the presence of our mother-in-law. All these are options that are open to us, but when we consciously think through the consequences, we might choose to do the socially acceptable behaviour at this point in time (or we might not).

For many people though, it's not like there is a fully formed True Self waiting in the wings to take centre stage. It is fine to hold on to the old, habitual False Self and gently experiment with trying out parts of what may or may not feel like our True Self until we get a fuller sense of who that person is. Think of it as being like trying on new costumes or clothes you would not normally pick from the rail, but might wear in the safety and privacy of your own home.

Here are some more ideas for things you might like to incorporate into your repertoire of True-Self behaviour. In a way, they are a bit like safety nets for the high-wire performer; which is you, daring to try something different.

Compassionate, with boundaries

Psychology professor Rachel Tribe was the first person to show me that you can be compassionate *with* boundaries. She was the course leader when I did a Masters degree in Advanced Counselling Psychology at the University of East London. She seemed to genuinely care about all the trials and tribulations, stresses and anxieties that are an integral part of the student lot. She was an empathic listener and would try hard to suggest a creative solution or compromise to her students' problems.

One day in particular sticks in my mind. It was a week before an assignment deadline and, predictably, a fair proportion of the class were panicking about getting their essays in on time. When it came to questions after the lecture that morning, several students started wheedling for a deadline extension. They had illnesses, house moves, sick parents, sick children, work complications ... Professor Tribe listened carefully to their various reasons, nodding sympathetically, then said a polite, but firm 'No'. If anyone had a genuine reason for lateness, they could fill in the relevant form and submit it to the office with supporting evidence (like a doctor's note). Otherwise, the deadline remained as it had been set.

I would definitely say it was a Gracious No (see page 126). It was also a very unpopular no, and some class members were furious. But she held firm, and her facial expression remained genuinely compassionate. I was so impressed that I have never forgotten it. It gave me the idea of a new possibility; a new way of being. But this also goes even further than learning the technique of how to say no graciously. Compassion with boundaries encompasses a way of thinking – a belief that 'I have the right to set boundaries' or 'Even if people dislike my decision, I am still a worthwhile and likeable person'.

Many Lovelies struggle to set boundaries and may have little experience of, or practice at, doing it. It is a phrase that is so frequently bandied about, yet one that is difficult to explain until you begin to experience it. Some clients have found it helpful to visualise something physical between them and others, to stop the feeling that the other person's emotions are penetrating into them, making it hard not to over-empathise and say yes, when they want to say no. Often this is something like a protective circle of light surrounding them (pick your own colour) or something more tangible (but transparent) like a Perspex bubble. One client visualised a high wall around her dream cottage, with tall iron gates and an intercom. Then, when her manipulative ex or intrusive mother called, she decided whether she was going to buzz them in or keep them out. This was transformative to her sense of self-esteem and safety.

Little victories, not partial failures

It is really important that you are compassionate to *yourself* on this journey of awareness and change. Remember, you are trying to change habits of belief and behaviour that are usually deeply ingrained from childhood – at least as hard as stopping biting your nails, hair twiddling or comfort eating.

Break things down into tiny steps and make sure you notice and reward your progress, however small it seems to your dismissive critical voices. Here is what Jessica has to say about her pace of progress:

Something from therapy that helped was realising that all these challenges we set together were complex tasks. Even the 'not smiling at someone when I don't want to'; I found that a big challenge, but one that I wanted to get on with. Being a perfectionist, I wanted to walk into work one day and be 100 per cent assertive in all situations and for people to immediately accept that. You helped me realise that small steps were needed and that I should think of them as little victories, as opposed to partial failures. So even if I said a 'Yes, but . . .' to someone instead of a resounding no, that was still a good thing and I could be kind to myself and think I've done well and that next time I could work on getting a bit more of this right.

Penny's date

Penny, the head teacher who has been married three times, largely because she didn't like to disappoint the men who fell in love with her (see page 172), sent an email to tell me how she got on with the behavioural experiment that she decided on at our workshop. If you remember, she was going on a date that night with a guy that she didn't have strong feelings for and wanted to try and be less enthusiastic and more 'compassionate with boundaries'. 'I found it really difficult,' she wrote. 'He had booked a table at an incredibly fashionable and expensive restaurant, so that immediately piled on the pressure and the guilt that I must be nice to him and couldn't possibly disappoint him.'

However, Penny had polished her tools (see Chapter Seven) before the date. She was particularly aware of her ability to be 'firm but kind' to problematic pupils and staff, and how these are transferable skills she could use once she had questioned the hidden Rigid Personal Rule from childhood (from her mother) that: A WOMAN MUST NEVER DISAPPOINT A MAN IN LOVE. So over an expensive and lavish meal, she looked him in the eye and was honest, but kind. 'You are a really lovely guy,' she said, 'but I have a lot going on in my life right now and it would be dishonest to take this any further.'

Penny wrote to me: 'I can honestly say that that is the first time in my life that I have done that with awareness and intent. It felt like a real turning point. He was upset, but it would have got a lot worse if I had allowed it to continue.'

MORE ABOUT THE LOVELIES WE'VE MET

Now I thought you might like to find out what happened to some of the other people who've been introduced in the book.

What happened to Hamish?

Hamish worked hard at accepting and integrating all parts of himself, including those he had labelled as his 'bad, dark side' (see page 48). By the time our therapy ended, Hamish didn't exactly like these parts of himself, but realised that they are part of who he is as a full, authentic human being and that it is only by showing these sides to others that he can have intimate, connected relationships. He has come a long way in making and maintaining fully connected friendships and this is largely due to having stopped limiting himself to the 'acceptable' Lovely sides of his personality and showing people some of the formerly taboo and hidden sides.

Hamish got a new job in a different part of the country and so ended his therapy. He felt he could reinvent himself in his new job and start how he meant to go on (his version of 'Never smile before Christmas', see page 122), rationing his wonderful smile, his charming jokes and his tendency to over-help.

He had begun to get in touch with the suppressed anger inside his body and identify the swirling adrenalin surge. He knew that this meant he was editing out a difficult thought (such as anger over the porridge saucepan), which he had begun to try to express – especially to his wife. But this change led to some conflict between them. I don't know whether they resolved that and moved forward together, or whether their relationship could not bear the new dynamic. I'd be misleading you if I pretended it was all happy endings, but I hope it is turning out as he wanted.

And a word of caution here: sometimes it does not feel safe to become more assertive in a relationship where your role has been passive. Sometimes the pressure to Change Back! (see page 168) can become violent. If this is the case, do whatever you need to feel safe: get help, call the police, go somewhere safe. Couple counselling may help, but only if you can put a mutual safety agreement in place first.

Amanda – the Lovely partner

After we created the Resentment Barometer (see page 46) together as a tool to help Amanda monitor the direct cost to her body of her 'over-giving' tendencies in her relationship with Simon, things began to shift in their dynamic. At first, the relationship went through a difficult phase where Simon seemed to become more distant and Amanda panicked. But, as I encouraged her to re-engage with hastily dropped friends and interests, the relationship seemed to become more balanced.

Harriet Lerner, author of *The Dance of Anger*, talks about people in intimate relationships falling into the habit of being the 'overfunctioner' or the 'underfunctioner'. Amanda had been overfunctioning like mad in the early days – and it had taken a heavy toll on her. She spent more time on her own and really enjoyed it; it helped her to recharge her batteries. She was less available for the late-night phone calls, but when she and Simon did talk she pushed herself to tell him about her health worries and a crisis at work and how she was feeling. She admitted that talking honestly about her feelings and vulnerabilities was probably the most difficult part for her, but it made them closer. 'Our relationship became more real, I suppose at the same time that I dared to be more real.'

INDIRA AND BEAR

Indira gave me this feedback a year after we had finished working together:

> I really like using the BEAR technique that you taught me (see page 187). It has been harder to apply with my family, as they are less receptive to me changing (or perhaps I am?). However, it has helped me to not see things in such a black and white way. It serves as a reminder to accept not only other people's opinions, but also my own, which is really hard for me. If I repeat BEAR to myself, I can not only eulogise others, I can also eulogise myself!
>
> So with my mother, I have used it when she told me how 'wrong' I was in an email following an argument with my sister. Rather than feeling wretched and blaming myself or sending a snide email back, I took a moment to think about it, had a rant to a friend and then accepted that she was probably in pain because two of her daughters were not speaking to each other and both complaining to her, which must be awful. My email back acknowledged her pain, told her what I needed from her and how she could help, but avoided going into details of

right and wrong between myself and my sister. The fact that she ignored this came as no surprise, but it shifted my thinking about myself and my own rights to have an opinion/emotional reaction without blaming myself or the other person!

I feel more confident in my communication with all my family members and better equipped to deal with them when I'm upset.

REBECCA'S STORY

I have included this story here because it shows how someone has used a combination of the ideas and strategies in this book to tackle a high-scoring item in her hierarchy of fear (see page 139).

Rebecca, who we met briefly earlier, is an inspiration to us all. She is a bright young woman who works in the media and who has bravely pursued change in the three sides of the triangle: thoughts, feelings and behaviour (see page 17) and has been rewarded with progress. She still has a lot of problems in her life to tackle, but is beginning to go about doing so in a different way.

After she landed her dream job (beating hundreds of other applicants), she was delighted that her boss took a personal interest in her and went the extra mile to help her settle in, show her the ropes and encourage her to flourish. 'I suppose I should have heeded the warning signs when he started telling me how special I was and gave me lots of personal attention, like taking me out for lunch,' Rebecca told me. But she, understandably, felt a mixture of flattered and grateful, and told her murmurings of unease to be quiet. Still, she was thrilled and relieved when she was promoted to a new role that was no longer under his team management. But – surprise, surprise – he still wanted to pursue their 'special' relationship and sent her endless emails suggesting inappropriate meetings after work – drinks and dinner. This caused Rebecca massively escalating stress and anxiety, basically making her life a misery. 'But I felt that somehow I had caused his fondness – that it was my fault in some way and that I couldn't be mean to him.' Rebecca had done a lot of work in therapy to build up her own sense of worth and value – she did the 'I love you' affirmation every day, plus the Three-good-things-a-day Diary and 'disappoint someone daily' (see pages 100, 101 and 164 respectively). But her ex-boss was someone she was too terrified to disappoint. We talked through a version of the Gracious No (see page 126) and role-played a script she could actually use. To start with, after a creative brainstorm without judgment (see page 152) threw up a whole host of options open to her, she chose the one that felt easiest and safest for the time being: moving her desk so she was not in his eyeline (he had been staring at her constantly).

Then one day she arrived at our session looking elated. Confident, free, no longer anxious. 'I met him!' she told me. 'After a series of pleading emails begging me to meet, I finally said yes – but only when I felt very strong after some extreme self-care' (she loved Cheryl Richardson's book about this).

'Wow,' I said. 'What happened?' 'Well, I used most of what we had talked about. I used the Gracious No and thanked him for meeting me, but I said very calmly and clearly that this was an inappropriate relationship for a senior male manager and a junior female member of staff and it had to end. He kept telling me how special I was and this had never happened to him before, but I used the stuck record and kept saying the same sentence. After ten minutes, I ended the conversation and left.' 'And now?' I asked. 'Well, I feel amazing! It has made me really happy and I feel free and empowered. Whatever he feels is his problem, but I know I did the right thing.'

MAKE YOUR OWN SOS CARD

Life is unpredictable, control is really just an illusion (think of natural disasters) and difficult and unfortunate things happen, often when we are least expecting them. And that's usually when we turn to old, unhelpful habits of thought, feeling and behaviour. In therapy this is called a relapse, and together we can put in place a plan to help you cope with this.

I have designed a template for an easy-to-use emergency intervention card. I have created it around the letters SOS – the emergency Morse code signal sent out in the war which stood for Save Our Souls. Pretty apt, I thought, as I know from my own and numerous clients' experience that things can feel pretty dark and desperate in a time of relapse.

Template for SOS card:

1. SPEAK: trusted person to call is ...

2. **** OFF!: best response to critical voices is ...

3. SOOTHE AND STRENGTHEN: favourite soothing and
   distracting activities are ...

On a small piece of card or paper that you can fit inside something you have easy access to (like your diary), fill in the spaces
with your own ideas. You may have a good idea of what some
of these are or you may need to give it some thought. Next to
the first 'S', list one or two supportive, trusted people you can
contact (no shoulds here – only those you feel you can safely
share your vulnerability with and they will not judge you or
offer too much advice). Then, next to the 'O', write your best
response to your critical voices when you are feeling strong
and confident. And finally, next to the second 'S', write down
some activities that help to soothe and strengthen you; this is
sometimes called 'healthy distraction', so try not to list
unhealthy things which will make you feel guilty.

Once you feel calmer, you can think about the next step, which
would be creative problem-solving. However, you usually need to
feel quite safe before you can access your problem-solving part of
the brain.

How Monika used her SOS card

Monika, who we first met in Chapter Two, had struggled all
her life with criticism from her parents. Her mother strongly

believed that 'criticism motivates children' and had not budged from this position despite reams of research evidence to the contrary, provided to her by her daughter when she was feeling brave.

Monika had been asked to appear on her local radio station to talk about a community project she was involved with. She (possibly inadvisably) told her parents when she would be interviewed. In retrospect, she told me, smiling ruefully, this should have set off her Arc of Redemption alert (see page 97), as she belatedly realised, she was probably, subconsciously, hoping for praise and affirmation from them.

The night after the broadcast – which had gone well – her father rang her about some other family arrangement. At the end of the call he casually said, 'I thought that other woman dominated the interview; you should have fought for your air-time.' That was it. Nothing else, no other comment. Monika said she felt totally winded. She ended the phone call as quickly as possible, poured herself a large glass of wine and burst into tears. Exhausted, she slumped on her sofa feeling depressed and demotivated.

Luckily, she remembered her SOS card. She got it from her wallet and started going through the steps. She texted her most trusted friend and they arranged to speak later. That alone calmed her down. She investigated her emotions and realised it was yet another Arc of Redemption ray of hope that felt snuffed out. Her inner child felt rejected and crushed, like she wanted to give up on everything. 'What is the point?' her critical dialogue was saying. 'You will never succeed at anything.' She looked at her card. Number 2: best response to critical voices is ... 'Bugger off you vultures. I am a success because I'm trying.'

Looking at her SOS card also reminded her that it might be nice to do some of the things that soothed her and lifted her mood. She ran a hot, scented bubble bath and put on some favourite music. Later, while she was putting on her softest pyjamas ready for an early night, she had what seemed like a breakthrough thought: she decided that if any of her family members mentioned the broadcast critically when they met the following day she would have a response prepared. She decided she would like to say: 'Look, I am just human like all of us and I felt vulnerable and nervous being interviewed on the radio. When you are critical I feel hurt, like any of you would.' Monika didn't know whether she would actually get the chance to be able to say this – or be able to say it if she got the chance; but having a 'script' was clarifying and calming. It made her feel more adult and empowered.

I imagine you'll want to know what happened to her. Well, she turned up at the family lunch the following day and no one mentioned the broadcast. Part of her was relieved and part of her was disappointed. After using her SOS format the night before, it didn't seem to matter that much any more. She realised that her father's criticisms were probably about his own fears and insecurities and she could extend a bit of compassion towards him.

SOS cards have been used by many other clients too; they have printed theirs out and put them in prominent but private places. Samantha printed hers out in different sizes, laminated them and put one on her bedroom mirror, one on the fridge and one in her wallet. Ella saved hers as a document on her computer and her smartphone. Susie sent copies to her two closest friends who she arranged to text with a special code word when things felt bad, as she knew her default coping mechanism was to retreat and isolate herself (as it had been when she was a child and had coped with conflict by going to her bedroom).

MY GIFT FROM THE BROKEN ARM: LESS, BETTER

Having used my own example to open the subject, people who attend my workshops often ask me, 'What happened after the broken arm? Are you cured now? Have you broken the Curse?' Well, I have and I haven't, I tell them. As with all our lives, it is a work in progress.

I no longer feel trapped in behaving in certain ways with most people. Those who go back furthest in my history I have found the most challenging and I still slip back, almost unconsciously, into my Little Miss Sunshine routine. But with most other people and situations I am much more aware of my options, and the fact that I can choose how I behave. So as the title of this chapter suggests, I can *choose* when I am kind, helpful, compassionate, entertaining, lively or whatever other Lovely behaviour I want to display; but I can also choose other behaviours without feeling I am a bad person who will be disliked and rejected. Some people *will* dislike and reject me, of course, but I feel that is now bearable and realistic and a small price to pay for looking after myself and tending to my needs.

I have faced other health challenges since the broken arm, which have also had a positive side. They have forced me to listen to what my body is telling me much more closely, and give it what it is asking for, within reason. When I am tired, I feel I can give myself permission to cancel things and rest. As a result, I now spend a lot more time in bed!

As you may have realised by now, I love creating little sayings – the shorter the better – which help me (and my clients) to remember how I want to live my life and guide the choices I make. As well as the many others mentioned in this book, my overriding phrase since the broken-arm epiphany has been 'Less, Better'. I apply this to all kinds of decluttering in my life, from chucking out stuff that isn't useful, doesn't fit or I'm not really fond of, to – like Liz (see page 51) – pruning down my social life. I now try to make time for those people with whom I genuinely feel a strong connection, feel safe enough to show my vulnerability to and be myself with, and to whom I can go for help.

This is the opposite of the '500-friends-on-Facebook' syndrome that makes many of my clients feel ashamed to have just a small handful of close, trusted friends. Having masses of virtual friends has become a contemporary *should,* that, like all other shoulds, can make us feel failures if we do not comply.

REGRETS OF THE DYING

Last month I was talking to a man at a friend's fiftieth birthday party about the Curse of Lovely. 'Oh, you should read this
book by a palliative care nurse,' he said. 'It's about the things
that dying people regret the most, and some of it definitely
sounds like your book. I think they regretted not being true to
themselves or something like that.' I duly bought the book,
The Top Five Regrets of the Dying by Bronnie Ware, and sure
enough, in her experience, regret number one was: I wish I'd
had the courage to live a life true to myself, not the life others
expected of me. And regret number three was: I wish I'd had
the courage to express my feelings, and not suppress them in
order to keep peace with others. (In case you're curious, regret
number two was: I wished I'd spent less time at the office and
more with my loved ones.)

As with any words of wisdom from the terminally ill, these
can help us live our lives *now* in different and hopefully
better ways. If one of our aims in life is to have no regrets,
then it is helpful to hear what is most commonly regretted.
It's not 'I wish I'd gone to the temporary secretary's leaving
drinks' or even, 'I wish I'd sailed around the world/bungee
jumped from the Grand Canyon'; it seems to come down to
having the courage to be who we really are, and let people
know what we really think (within reason) – especially those
we love.

REDRAW YOUR PICTURE

Remember the exercise I introduced in Chapter Three? You were invited to write, in the lines emanating from the Lovely's head, the qualities that you want the world to see. Then, bubbling underneath, within the triangular gown, were the parts of you that you seek to hide from the world.

Now we're going to encapsulate your journey of breaking the Curse of Lovely in a new drawing. This is how you would like to be. You cannot achieve it overnight; like all the most rewarding journeys, it is slow and beset with distractions, unexpected potholes, diversions and detours. But gradually, you will no longer feel cursed, but blessed that you have the skills and qualities to be Lovely – not only to others, but to yourself.

On the following page you will see how I redrew my own picture. In the emanating lines I have: straightforward, honest, fun, energetic, serious, compassionate, clear boundaries (but all when I choose; no compulsion to act in a certain way); inside (no longer simmering away, but tucked away with care) I have: vulnerability and fears – to be shared mindfully with 'safe' people only.

In an ideal world maybe nothing would be shameful or suppressed and we would all be fully human and fully authentic. But while we live in this world, at this time, this new picture is the realistic self I am aiming for: a combination of my true self, with a bit of Winnicott's 'Healthy False Self' (see page 194) there for safety. When I manage to do something different – like say no to a difficult person – then I try and praise myself, maybe even give myself a small treat as a reward.

You too will manage to do something different, I know you will. I have great faith in the amazing capacity of human beings to courageously experiment and break old patterns. Once you begin, you will be empowered and emboldened by your successes. You will discover that one safe, compassionate step at a time you can go out and realise your full range of wonderful qualities, quirks and strengths. You too can break the Curse of Lovely and be everything you were born to be.

REFERENCES

CHAPTER ONE

Lerner, H., *The Dance of Anger* (Element, 1990)
Beck, A. T., *Cognitive Therapy and the Emotional Disorders* (IUP, 1975)

CHAPTER TWO

Greene, C., *New Toddler Taming: A Parents' Guide to the First Four Years* (Vermillion, 2001)
Bowlby, J., *Child Care and the Growth of Love* (Penguin, 1953)
Winnicott, D. W., *Playing and Reality* (Penguin, 1971)
Rogers. C., *On Becoming a Person: A Therapist's View of Psychotherapy* (Constable, 1961)

CHAPTER THREE

Dickson, A., *A Woman in Your Own Right* (Quartet, 1982)
Faludi, S., *Backlash: The Undeclared War Against American Women* (Crown, 1991)
Hendrix, H., *Getting the Love You Want* (Pocket Books, 1993)

CHAPTER FOUR

The *Guardian*, 7 January 2012

CHAPTER FIVE

Desert Island Discs, BBC Radio Four, 2 March 2012
Beck, A. T., *Cognitive Therapy and the Emotional Disorders* (IUP, 1975)
Harris, R., *The Happiness Trap* (Robinson, 2008)
Dickson, A., *A Woman in Your Own Right* (Quartet, 1982)

CHAPTER SIX

The *Guardian*, 3 February 2012
Richardson, C., *The Art of Extreme Self-Care* (Hay House, 2009)
Cameron, J., *The Artist's Way* (Pan, 1995)

CHAPTER SEVEN

Kelly, G. A., *A Theory of Personality: Psychology of Personal Constructs* (Norton, 1955)
Mehrabian, A., *Silent Messages: Implicit Communication of Emotions and Attitudes* (Wadsworth, 1971)
Dickson, A., *Difficult Conversations* (Piatkus, 2004)

CHAPTER NINE

Lerner, H., *The Dance of Anger* (Element, 1990)

CHAPTER TEN

Sampson, V., *Tantra: The Art of Mindblowing Sex* (Vermillion, 2002)

CHAPTER ELEVEN

Winnicott, D. W., *Playing and Reality* (Penguin, 1971)
Lerner, H., *The Dance of Anger* (Element, 1990)
Ware, B., *The Top Five Regrets of the Dying* (Hay House, 2012)

FURTHER READING

Here are some books that myself and my clients have found helpful:

PARENTING

Faber, A; and Mazlish, E., *How To Talk So Kids Will Listen and Listen So Kids Will Talk* (Avon, 1982)
Faber, A; and Mazlish, E., *Siblings Without Rivalry* (Avon, 1987)
Stadlen, N., *What Mothers Do: Especially When it Looks Like Nothing* (Piatkus, 2005)
Greene, C., *New Toddler Taming: A Parents' Guide to the First Four Years* (Vermillion, 2001)

RELATIONSHIPS

Hendrix, H., *Getting the Love You Want* (Pocket Books, 1993)
Hendrix, H., *Keeping the Love You Find* (Pocket Books, 1995)
Lerner, H., *The Dance of Anger* (Element, 1990)
Lerner, H., *The Dance of Connection* (Piatkus, 2001)
Perel, E., *Mating in Captivity* (HarperCollins, 2006)
Sampson, V., *Tantra: The Art of Mindblowing Sex* (Vermillion, 2002)

SELF-HELP AND THOUGHT-PROVOKING

Brown, B., *I Thought It Was Just Me (but it isn't): Telling the Truth about Perfectionism, Inadequacy and Power* (Gotham Books, 2007)

Cameron, J., *The Artist's Way* (Pan, 1995)

Chaplin, J., *Deep Equality: Living in the Flow of Equalizing Rhythms* (O Books, 2008)

Harris, R., *The Happiness Trap* (Robinson, 2008)

Richardson, C., *The Art of Extreme Self-Care* (Hay House, 2009)

Ware, B., *The Top Five Regrets of the Dying* (Hay House, 2012)

ASSERTIVENESS

Dickson, A., *A Woman in Your Own Right* (Quartet, 1982)

Dickson, A., *Difficult Conversations* (Piatkus, 2004)

RESOURCES

UK

HOW TO FIND A THERAPIST

The British Psychological Society (BPS) can help you find a
counselling psychologist in your area. For more details see
www.bps.org.uk or phone 01662 549568

The British Association for Counselling and Psychotherapy (BACP)
has a database of qualified psychotherapists and counsellors in the
UK. For more details see www.bacp.co.uk or phone 0870 443
5252

MINDFULNESS

I would strongly recommend doing an eight-week mindfulness
course, similar to that mentioned in Chapter Five, which is
approximately 2 hours per week and teaches the approach
together with breathing and meditation exercises.

Bangor University has a Centre for Mindfulness Research and
Practice and can provide information on different courses and
training. For more details see: www.bangor.ac.uk/mindfulness

A linked site: www.bemindful.co.uk can help you find your nearest eight-week course.

An excellent book is *Mindfulness: A Practical Guide to Finding Peace in a Frantic World*, by Mark Williams and Danny Penman (Piatkus, 2011). This takes you through an eight-week course and includes a CD of guided meditations.

AUSTRALIA AND NEW ZEALAND

You can find a psychologist via the New Zealand Psychological Society at www.psychology.org.nz

The Australian Psychological Society can be found at www.psychology. org.au

For information about mindfulness courses see www.mindfulness. org.au and www.mindfulness-training.co.nz

INDEX

Note: page numbers in *italics* refer to diagrams.